The time between the day and the evening
is one of seductive, mysterious enchantment
when thoughts are spurred to the creation of desire.

Ideas, places, people and things
can be subtly turned in to
flirtatious venues of passion and ambiance.

Venture

if you dare

into.......

Other books by Julia Trops

Simplicity in Mind - catalog for the Livessence Society for Figurative Artists and Models
2009 Okanagan Erotic Art Show Catalog
Lauren - Sensuality of Form
Donnalee (forthcoming)

The Edge of Night

2011 Okanagan Erotic Art Show Catalog

Ex Nihilo Vineyards
31 August - 28 September 2011

http://www.okanaganeroticartshow.com

Published by Julia Trops ISBN 978-0981336329

Designed and compiled by Julia Trops

Font: title page: Cracked
Paragraphs: Premier Garamond Pro

This book is dedicated to the artists in this catalog. Thank you for putting on a great show:

Angelika Jaeger, Brian Peterson, Brittany Falk, Calvin Bradbury, Carol Schlosar, Brazen
Edwards-Hager, Colm McCarthy, Dan McCormack, David Dixon, Devorah Ticha, Erin Foggoa,
Gail Marie Kern, Gary Mitchell, Greg Riley, Jaine Buse, Jennifer Burrows, Jim Britton, Jim Duvall, Johann Wessels,
John Schnurrenberger, Joyce Krenn, Karen Rempel, Karen Rudolph, Karla Warkotsch, Kendi Clearwater,
Koreena Lane, Laura F Klopp, Lauri Copeman, Lesley Harris, Lisa Figueroa, Lisolette Gilcrest,
Marissa Brown, Patricia Feist, Ronnie Olson, Roxi Sim Hermsen, Ryan Robson, Sandra Windsor,
Sea Dean, Sharon Rose, Shirley Leswick, Tina Aziz-Siddiqui, Trina Ganson

And to Jeff and Decoa Harder of Ex Nihilo,
you have vision, and I am glad to know you and to work with you.

To my husband Chris and best friend and supporter, I love you!

Preface

The Okanagan Erotic Show emerged in 2007, fellow artists Lauren Wilson, Angela Hansen and myself were talking about having an art show that was a bit more exciting than the usual run of the mill life drawing exhibitions. We were having a sip (or two, maybe more, I can't remember) of wine while manning the Livessence booth at one of the local art shows, and noticed there were many people who would barely glance at the nudes on display. Censorship about what was "proper" had reared its ugly head. Knowing full well that erotic is perceived individually, we wanted to shake things up. We wanted to have some FUN!

The first show, "Blush, what makes you?" at the Rotary Centre for the Arts (RCA) in 2008 was a huge success, but as you can imagine, as the RCA is a public building, there were a few complaints. The interest, though, was definitely there. In 2009, Angela went on to have her first child, and Lauren went traveling in Asia, so that year, I carried on my own, and have since. "Raw......Whispers" was at A. Woodside Design Gallery, and that year I created the first catalog. I realized how important that record seemed to be to each artist.

2010 saw a bit of rough bumps and grinds, but that experience showed me where we, the Okanagan artists, were in terms of comfort level and where we, the public, were in terms of artistic support and adventure. Finally, "Seduce Me" was held at Ex Nihilo Vineyards. I was overwhelmed by the attendance at the opening night, and the tremendously positive comments on the show throughout its run, by both artists and attendees.

Opening the Call to the United States in 2010 was the right thing to do. Moving the show to an open accepting environment at the winery out of Kelowna was the right thing to do. There is no catalog for 2010, as it was all timing or rather lack of time, due to the circumstances experienced, but hopefully there will be catalogs for years going forward.

This year, 2011, there are about half Canadian artists, and half American. I am thrilled with the content and the scope of expression, and know the show is definitely on the right track. Because I had to turn so many overseas artists away this year, for 2012, the show will be open worldwide.

Introduction

Erotic expression is personal. What one may find wildly outlandish, another may say is tame. In the last four years that I have put on this show, what has been constant is that more females have participated, and more females submitted feminine nudes than male (or even any other subject). You are probably not surprised either. This year though, the number of male artists has increased substantially, and the quality of work, I daresay, will appeal to both sexes.

Some of the expressions contained within this book are not female nudes, though some are, they are not blatantly in the throes of orgasm, though some are, they are not just life drawing, though some are. For some, eroticism is fantasy, it is thought, it is suggestion, for others, it is the obvious visuals, the tools, the deed.

A note about the female form in art - ask any artist about the female in art, and many will say that they are objectified (the nude, not the artist). I disagree. I think the artist IS objectified. Just kidding! I think that if a viewer sees a nude and feels that the nude is an object, that tells me more about the viewer than the nude. We live in an artistic stage of life where both the viewer and the artist calls the shots, and both are right. The nudes in this catalog are not victims or objects... unless YOU say they are.

Eroticism can only be a solitary activity - you may choose to share it with another but only you can perceive what is erotic - only you can label it so or not. Only you can label a nude form as being too risque, or too boring, It all has to do with your own interpretation, your own experience, your own psychology.

Many of the artists you will see in this show are putting themselves out on a limb - they are taking a chance in showing work that perhaps no one has seen before - they are dancing naked in front of you. There may also be some artists in this show that are more leaders in this field and have exhibited many times before in this subject area. What all are giving you however, is vulnerability, and a window in to their secret world. Whether new or not, I applaud the courage that these artists have, and their self-confidence, and I thank them for sharing that with us at the Edge of Night.

About the wine.... Night

Night....a forgotten story in the phenomenon of wine.

Ex Nihilo Night was created in honor of the mysterious balance the night brings to our vineyards. The cool night air off the Mountain Range and Lakes lowers the vineyard temperature just enough to slow down the ripening process to develop richer fruit with more complexity.

VINTAGE DESCRIPTION:
The 2007 season started with warm weather early in the spring, which was followed by a cooler period through mid-May but gave way to a beautiful hot Okanagan summer. The warmth allowed the grapes to reach their full ripeness potential. A cooler September further intensified the fruit flavours, added complexity and resulted in good acidity.

TASTING NOTES:
The 2007 Night is a blend of 50% Merlot, 25% Cabernet Sauvginon and 25% Cabernet Franc. The wine is showing wonderful rich fruit aromas of raspberry, cherry and black currant highlighted by white pepper. This elegant Bordeaux style wine is perfectly balanced with soft velvety chocolate tannins and a finish that lasts as long as a clear Okanagan summer night. 20 months French Oak.

RELEASE DATE:
September 1, 2010

WINEMAKER: Jim Faulkner

http://exnihilovineyards.com/night_2007.php

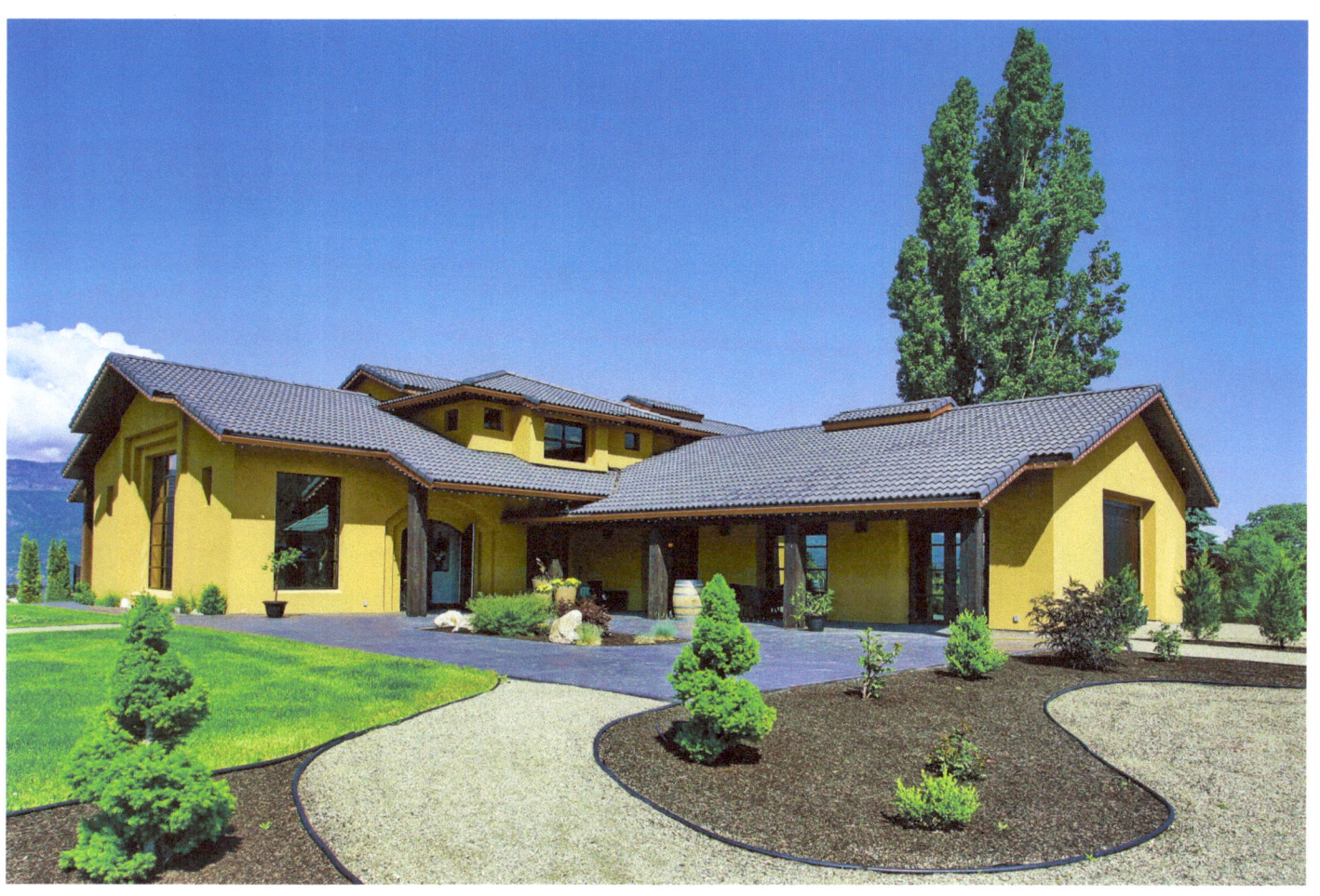

Ex Nihilo Vineyards
1525 Camp Road
Lake Country, BC

http://www.exnihilovineyards.com

Proprietors:
Jeff and Decoa Harder, Jay and Twila Paulson

The Artists

Angelika Jaeger
Brian Peterson
Brittany Falk
Calvin Bradbury
Carol Schlosar
Brazen Edwards-Hager
Colm McCarthy
Dan McCormack
David Dixon
Devorah Ticha
Erin Foggoa
Gail Marie Kern
Gary Mitchell
Greg Riley
Jaine Buse
Jennifer Burrows
Jim Britton
Jim Duvall
Johann Wessels
John Schnurrenberger
Joyce Krenn
Julia Trops
Karen Rempel
Karen Rudolph
Karla Warkotsch
Kendi Clearwater
Koreena Lane

Laura F Klopp
Lauri Copeman
Lesley Harris
Lisa Figueroa
Lisolette Gilcrest
Marissa Brown
Patricia Feist
Ronnie Olson
Roxi Sim Hermsen
Ryan Robson
Sandra Windsor
Sea Dean
Sharon Rose
Shirley Leswick
Tina Aziz-Siddiqui
Trina Ganson

Angelika Jaeger

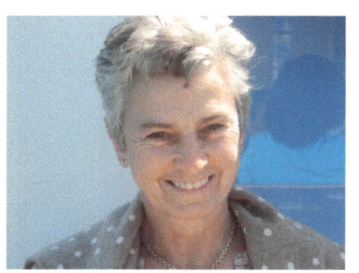

As a student of the arts and of life, I am always intrigued by what presents itself. The human body is an easy model from which to draw, not only in the literal sense, but even more so in the spiritual. I hope I will always stay hungry to learn, on my journey of life, to discover what is revealed around each corner and remain forever seduced and tempted by what life presence to me.

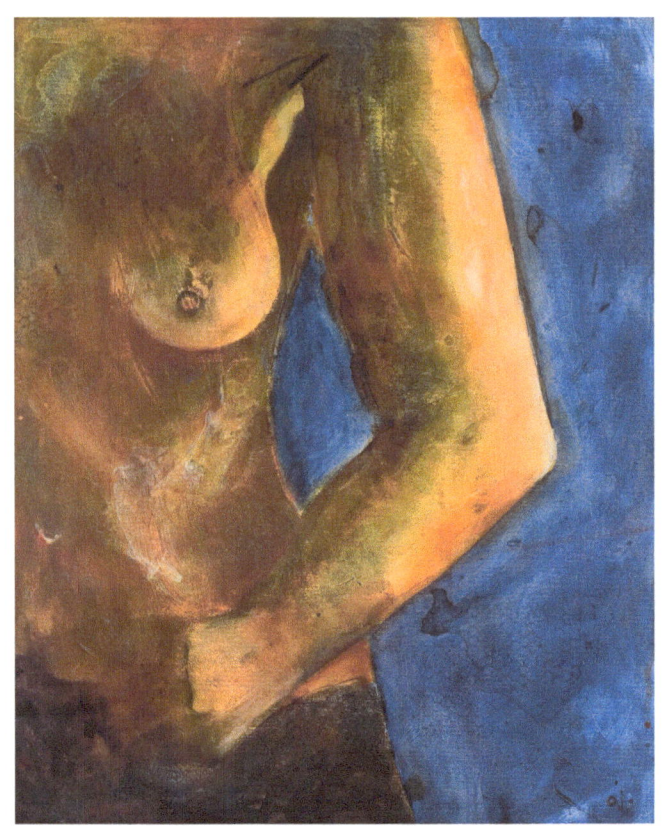

Within Her
Angelika Jaeger
18"x24"
Mixed Media

Strong, assured, knowing,
powerful and tough...
on the outside...
soft, gentle, smooth,
welcoming, and embracing....
trusting to hold on 'Within Her'

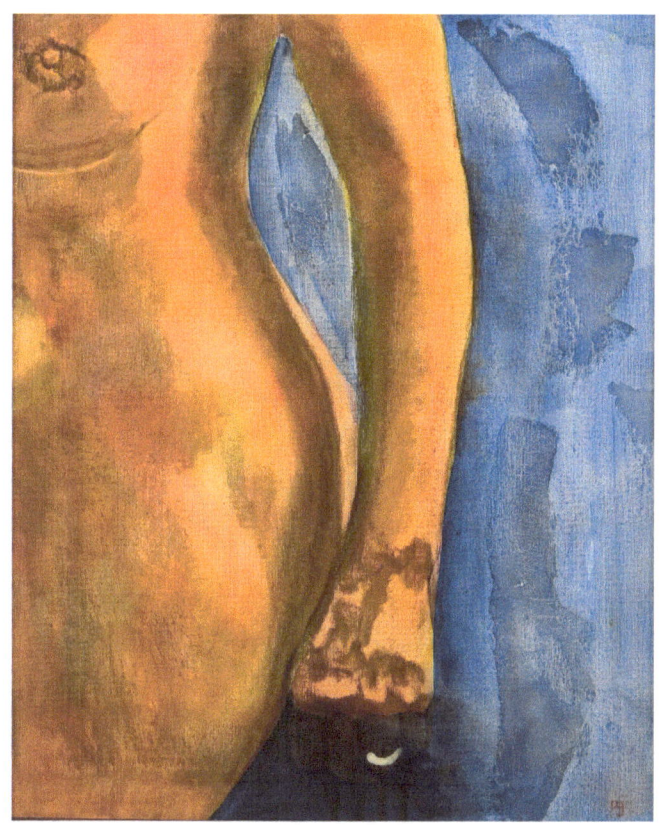

Gently Assured
Angelika Jaeger
16"x20"
Mixed Media

Standing within,
fleeing the doubts,
excepting the now,
facing the dark,
assuring the thoughts
being in the transition

Brazen Edwards-Hager

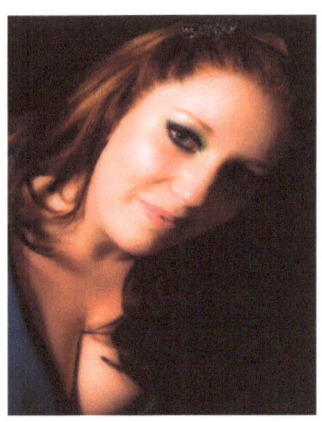

Brazen Edwards-Hager was born in Edmonton, the 29th of May, 1976. As a young girl it became apparent to her family that she had the innate aptitude for drawing so her Grandmother mentored that ability and enrolled her in numerous classes at the Edmonton Art Gallery. She was eventually encouraged her to attend high school at the newly developed Victoria School of Performing and Visual Arts, where she received formal training in fine art, set design and construction.

She later enrolled in the BA Criminology Program at the University of Alberta where she was given special permission to take Art Fundamentals as a component of her Bachelor of Arts degree and concentrated on painting, printmaking, sculpture and drawing. She later went on to pursue a career with the Royal Canadian Mounted Police and relocated to the Okanagan in 2009 with her Fiance' and teenage twin boys.

After a heartfelt decision Brazen realized her one true regret in life was putting her art aside for so long, so with the encouragement of her family, she took the initiative and began devoting herself to her Art full time. Although she has established a reputation with Wildlife, her subject matter also includes Still Life, Landscapes, Figurative and Portraits. She feels it's important to push herself as an Artist and to explore the boundaries - never being afraid to try new and controversial approaches to art.

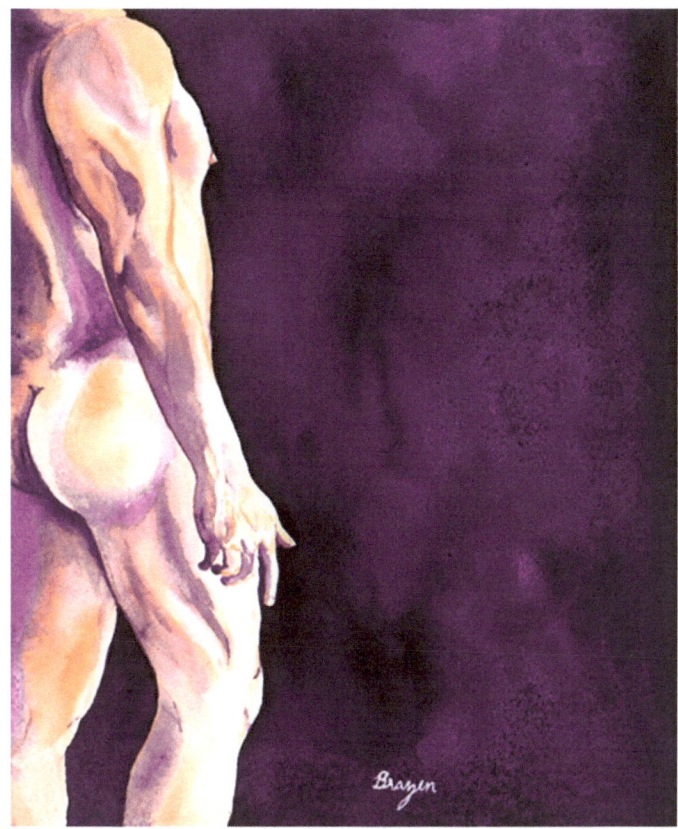

Temptation
Brazen Edwards-Hager
20"x17.5"
Watercolour

"Temptation" is an expression objectifying the male form
where you capture the essence and visualize a fragment of
his sex appeal.

Brian Peterson

Brian Peterson lives in Kelowna BC and is a member of the Livessence Society of Figurative Artists.

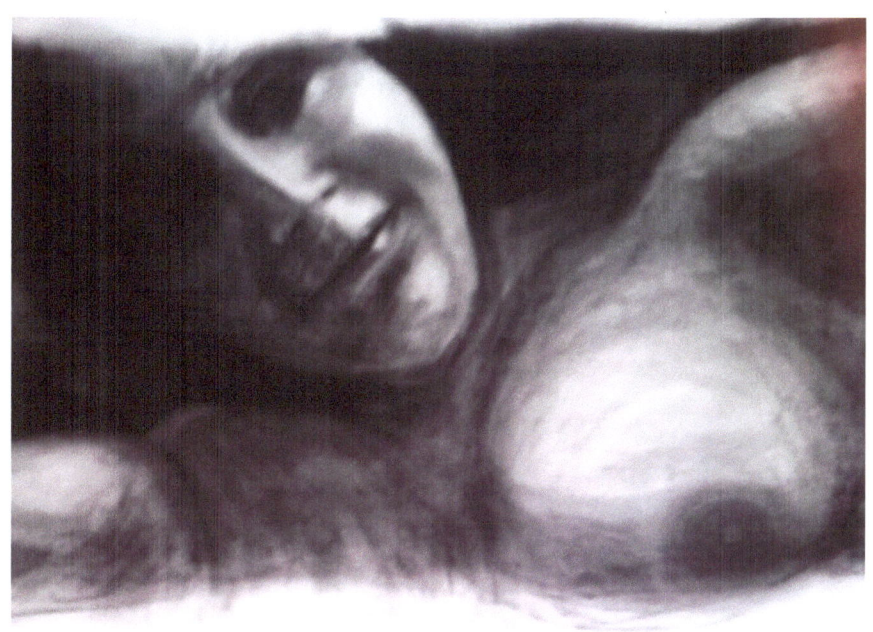

Reina de Cuba
Brian Peterson
18"x24"
Charcoal

We're alive at the edge of the night
Moonlit skin warm
Weight is light on you

Brittany Falk

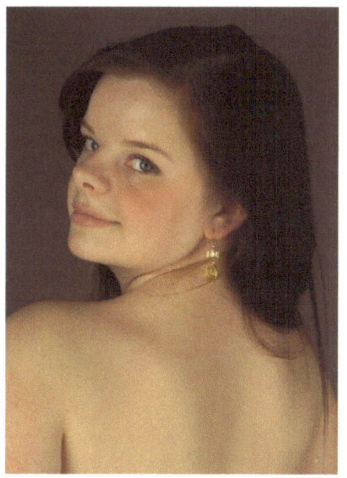

I have always had a love affair with the body. Although this has taken many artistic forms it is most obvious in my painting. I find the variables of the human body fascinating. The nude is incredibly prevalent in art history and it continues to captivate people. I want to paint as many different models as many ways as I can imagine. I think the uniqueness of each body should be celebrated and I try to pick out the parts of people that interest me and emphasize those in my paintings.

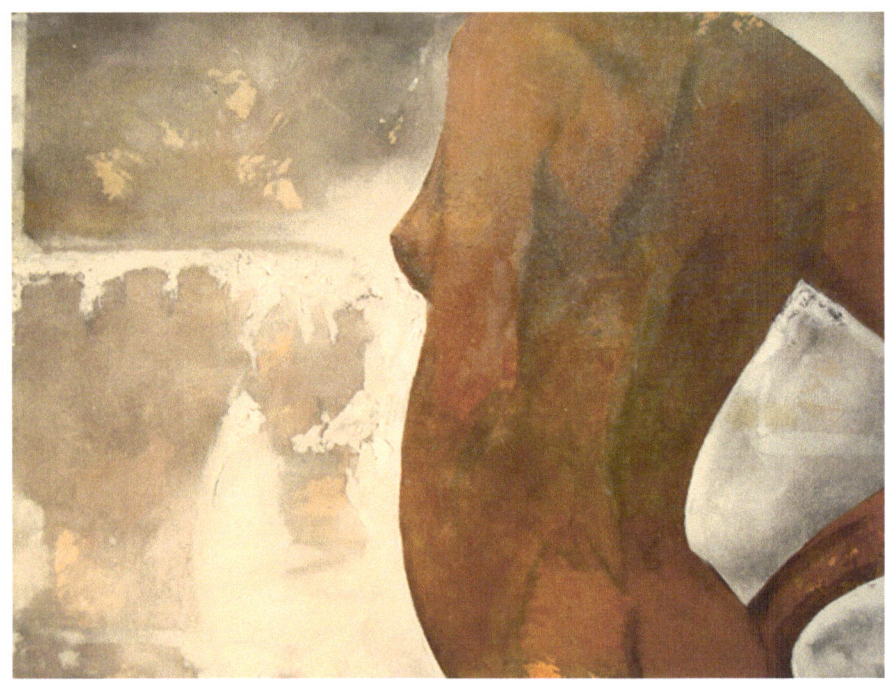

Silhouette 1
Brittany Falk
36"x48"
Watercolour and Acrylic on Canvas

On the edge of night things become veiled. It's that sliver of time where the eye can't quite adjust. What the eye can't perceive, the mind creates.

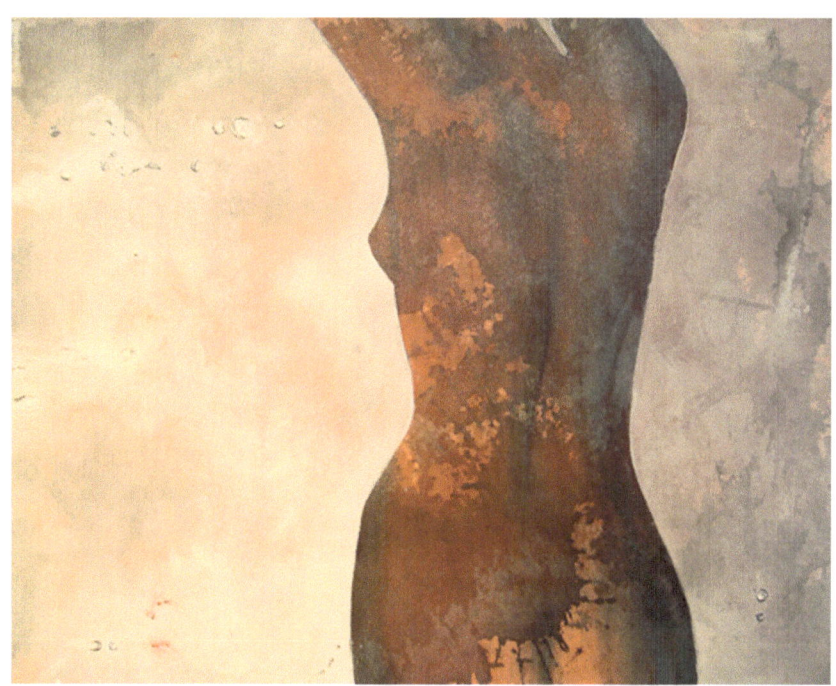

Silhouette 3
Brittany Falk
36"x48"
Watercolour and Acrylic on Canvas

At dusk, you can never really know what the silhouettes in the distance are.

Calvin Bradbury

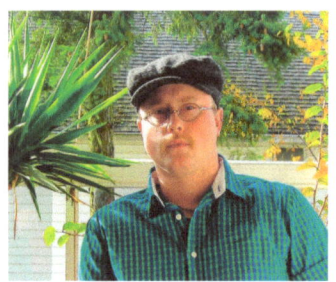

Calvin is a self-taught artist originally from Nova Scotia who has lived in West Coast Canada for many years. While we can accept that the technical development of his paintings as progressive, to believe that Bradbury has not professionally studied is a phenomena. Spending time on the margins of society in some periods of his life, art has carried Bradbury through the vicissitudes of the peripheral. The attitude toward his work is to avoid mainstream style and ideas and realize his own vision.

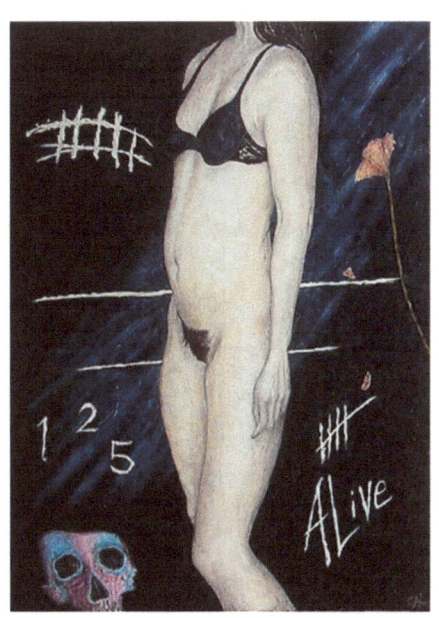

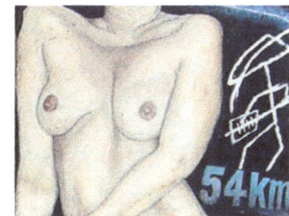

Carnival of Time
Calvin Bradbury
24"x18" and 9"x12"
diptych
Oil on Canvas

A work regarding the transition of time in an engagement, as well as much
time spent apart for the reasons of circumstances of life.

Carol Schlosar

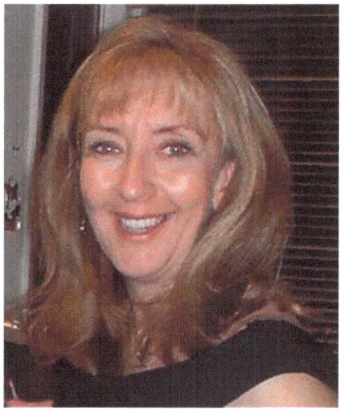

While fascinated by the mind- body connection, Carol Schlosar has always been captured by the sensuous lines of the human body. The curve of the hips, the sweep of the shoulder, the arc of the neck- she just couldn't resist "The Edge of Night".

Musician, teacher, composer, author, Sicamous artist, Carol Schlosar was always "making marks", but it wasn't until 4 years ago that she chose to explore her art in a serious way. Carol's adventures in expression have led her into acrylic, oil, pencil and clay. Willing to try everything, she dives into the creative process with excitement.

Bold shapes and colors. Ambiguous, textural abstracts that play with simple shapes and shadow. Her prolific body of work articulates her passion and playfulness.

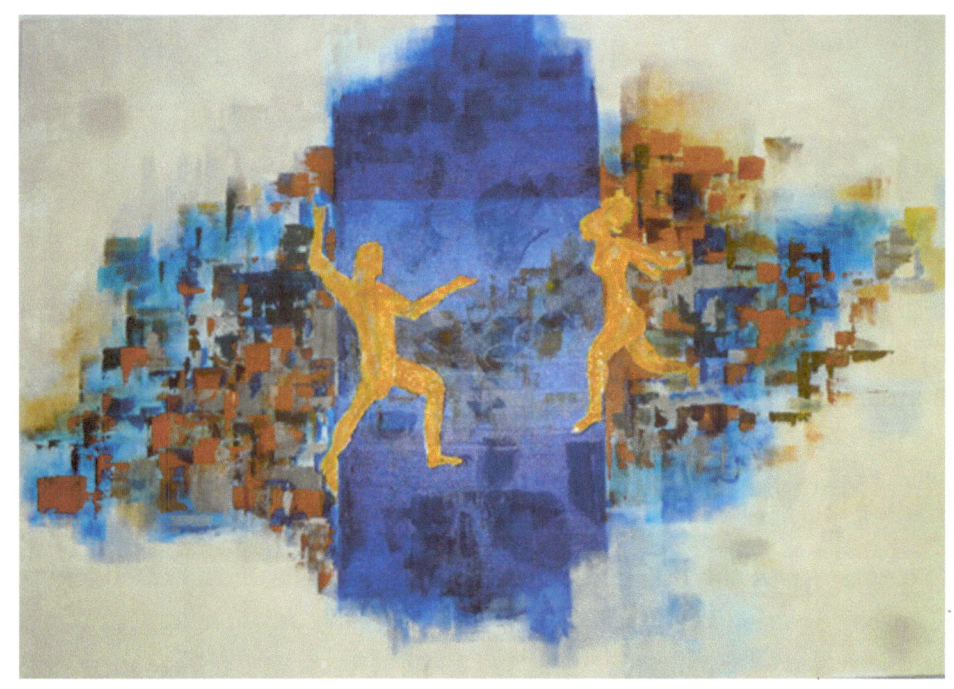

Dance
Carol Schlosar
24"x36"
Acrylic

Outthrust arm, silently he commands. Willingly, shyly, joyously she answers.
It's all about the Dance.

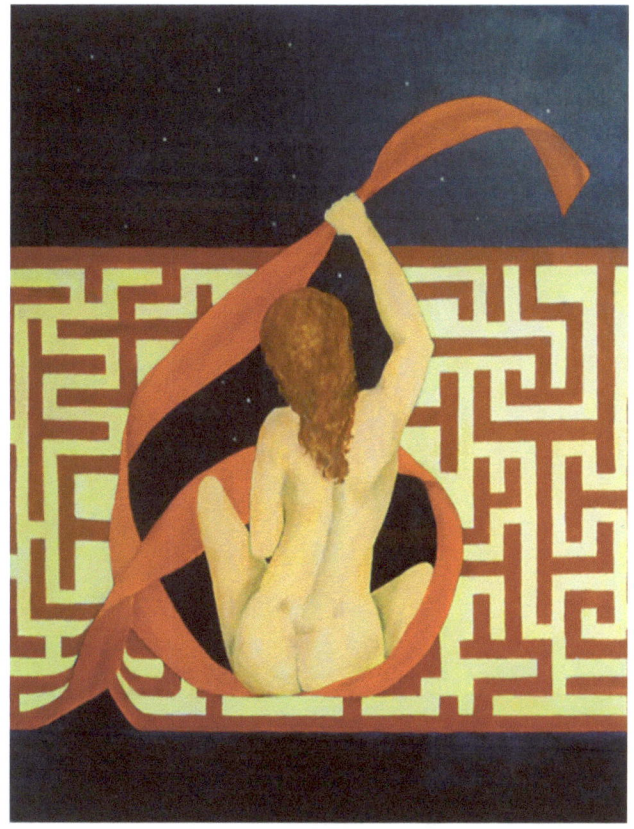

The Ribbon
Carol Schlosar
30"x24"
Acrylic

Unwind me.....Unbind me.......Recline me

Colm McCarthy

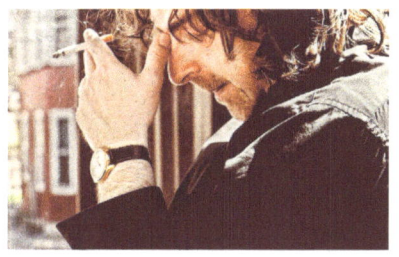

I am an Irish photographer and artist currently based in the US. I began doing nudes as it was cheaper than using elaborate costumes, and it's kind of stuck. I don't consider myself a "nude" or "erotic" photographer. But many people think otherwise, so I suppose I am. I regularly show my work nationally and internationally. This year it seems to be mainly nudes, so it would appear I am my own worst enemy.

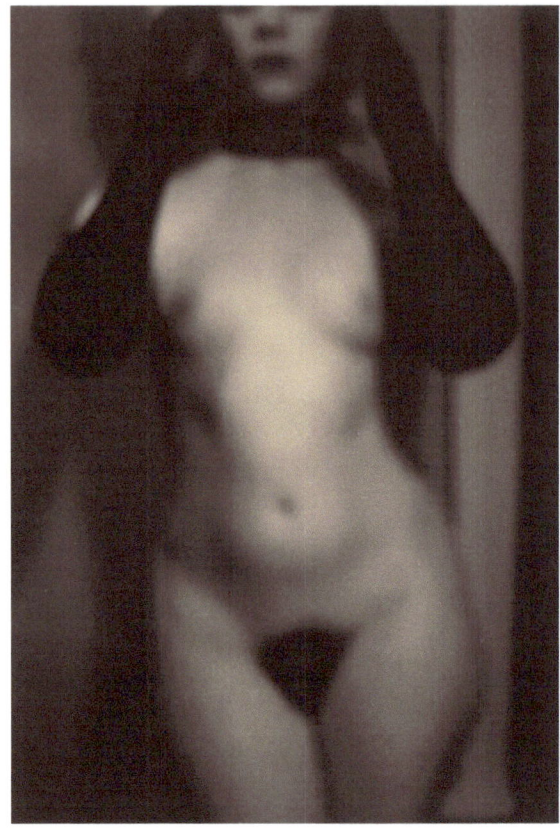

The Nun
Colm McCarthy
Archival pigment print on watercolor paper

Evening formal attire is never complete without
gloves, a powdered wig and a dog collar.

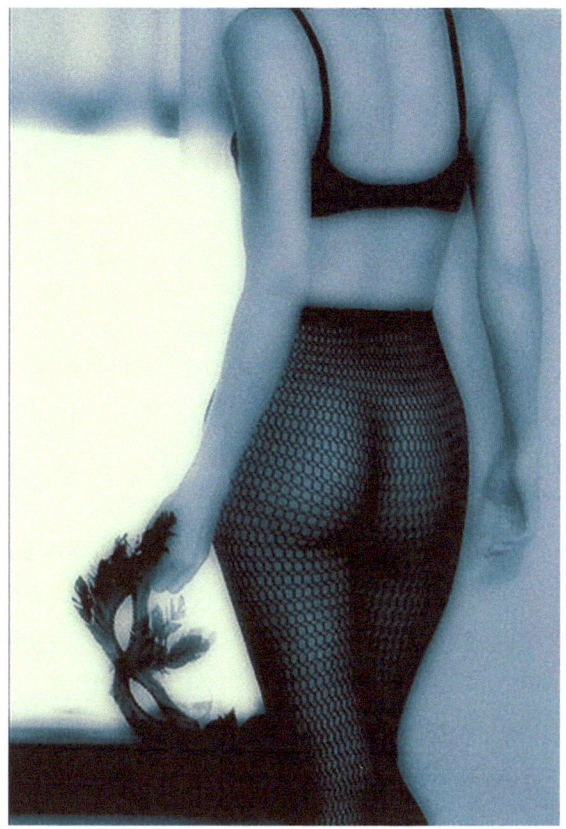

For Liz Mares
Colm McCarthy
Archival pigment print on watercolor paper

As the sun begins to fade, the mask comes off.

Dan McCormack

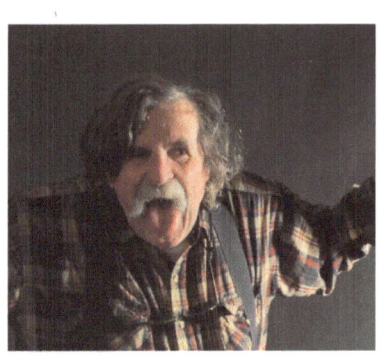

I studied Photography from 1962 - 1967 at the Institute of Design in Chicago and at the School of the Art Institute of Chicago from 1967 to 1970. I began photographing the nude with Wendy, my wife, while in graduate school. Then for over forty years I explored various techniques and processes while photographing the nude as a central theme. In 1982, I won a NYSCA-CAPS Photography Fellowship with a series of infrared nude images that I made of Wendy. With that series, I produced a monograph, "BODY LIGHT-Passages in a Relationship" in 1989. In 1998 I began to work with pinhole photography. In 2009, I won the Ultimate Eye Foundation's grant for Figurative Photography with my pinhole camera imagery and had my work featured in an exhibition at the Peninsula Museum of Art in Belmont, CA. From January to February 2010 I had a solo show at the Photography Center of the Capitol District in Troy, NY. I showed over fifty images from ten diverse series made from 1990 to 2010.

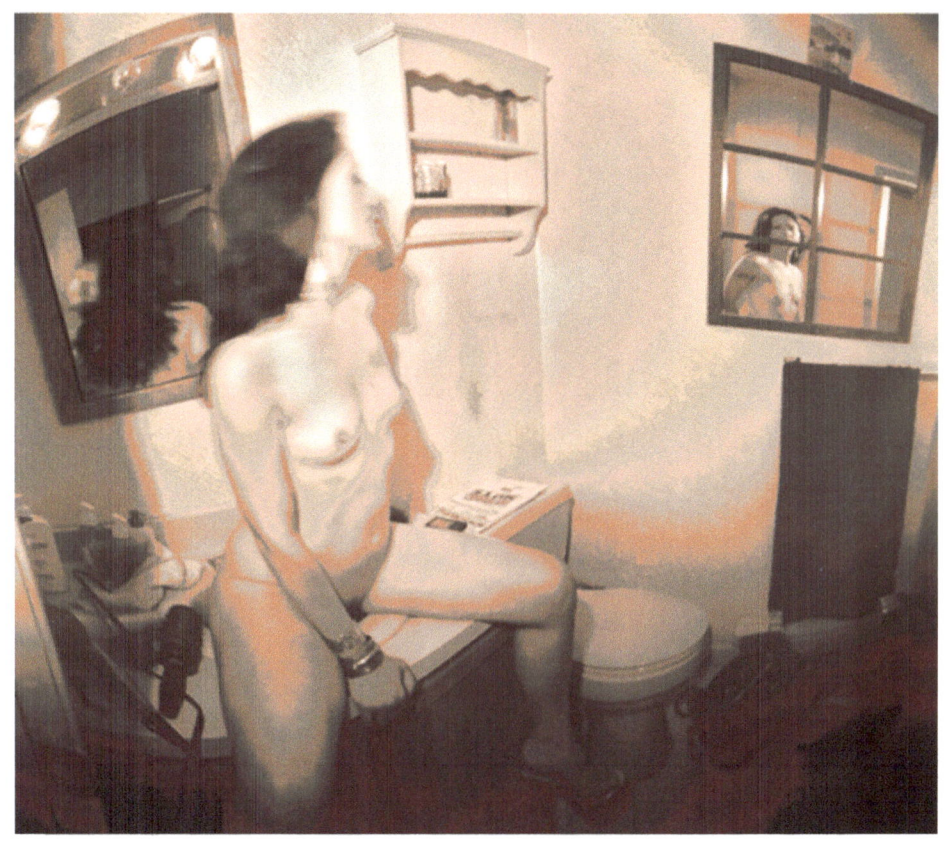

Ithaca_J_8-15-09--11AB
Dan McCormack
20"x16"
Pinhole Camera Digital pigment print

Ithaca_J_8-15-09--11AB was shot at her boyfriend's house.
The three of us talked and laughed until ten or so shots that I set up with Ithaca
in different rooms in the house.

David Dixon

A former art director and graphic designer, David's illustrations have appeared on book and magazine covers, and his international exhibition record includes venues such as the National Computer Art Invitational Exhibition and the Red Clay Survey at the Huntsville Museum of Art. He has received awards from the Colored Pencil Society of America and the 25th Educational Advertising Awards competition. He has presented at national conferences such as the University College Design Association (UCDA) on the subject of art in virtual worlds.

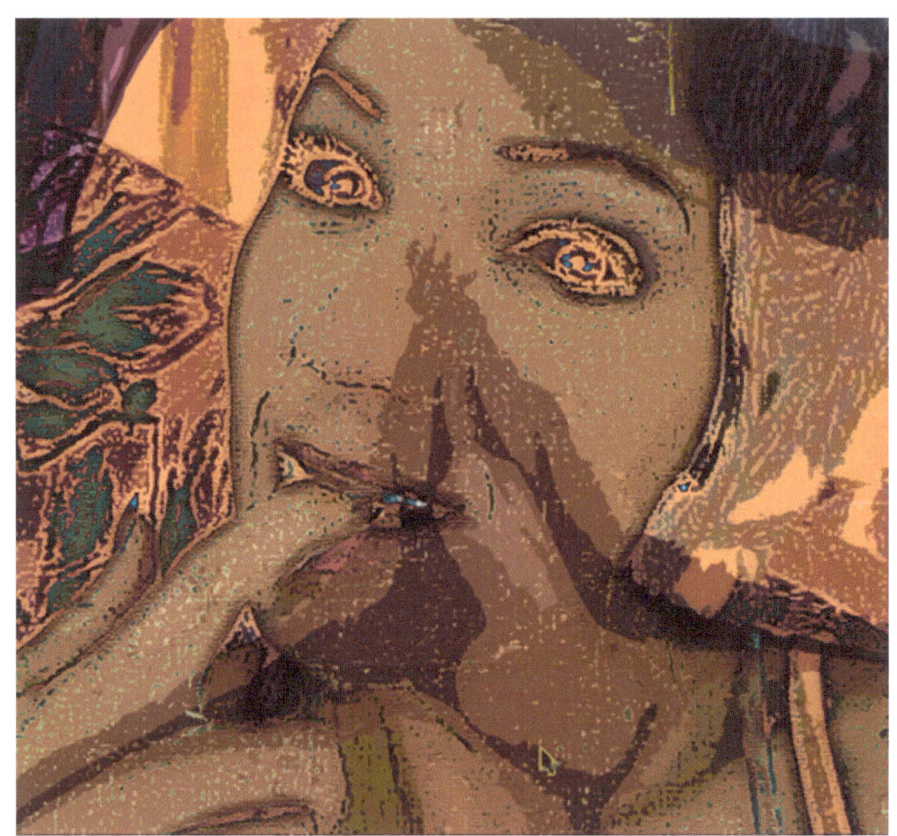

Late Afternoon
David Dixon
12"x11"
digital media

Layers of light and shadow depict an erotic fantasy.

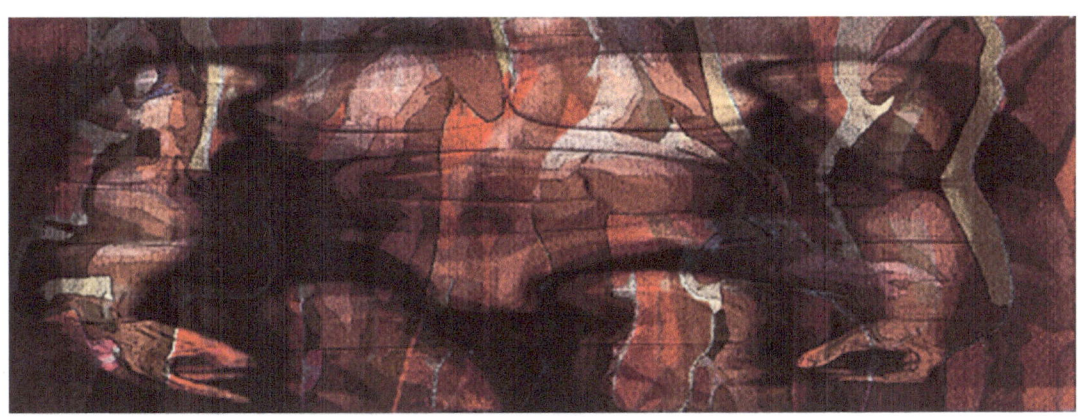

Show and Tell
David Dixon
18"x6.75"
digital media

Don't be a Weiner. Too much interplay with internet erotica can lead to your downfall.

Devorah Ticha

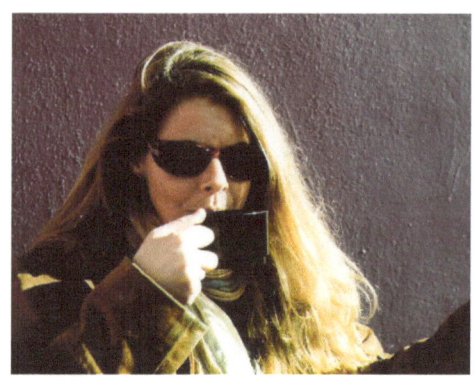

A Letter to The Under the Bed Monster

You are beautiful. I see your back, your legs, strong face. And gentle nature. There is a grounding within you that I like the feel of. I want to paint you. I want to paint your back, your arms, legs, shoulders, and press them onto a sheet of white cotton that I can put on the ceiling of my bedroom. A piece of art, as you are Monster. I believe .The wind catching the folds of the fabric, rippling above my head and body as I sleep. To wake up to, under. I imagine that. But you cannot come out from the bed, Monster. Good night.

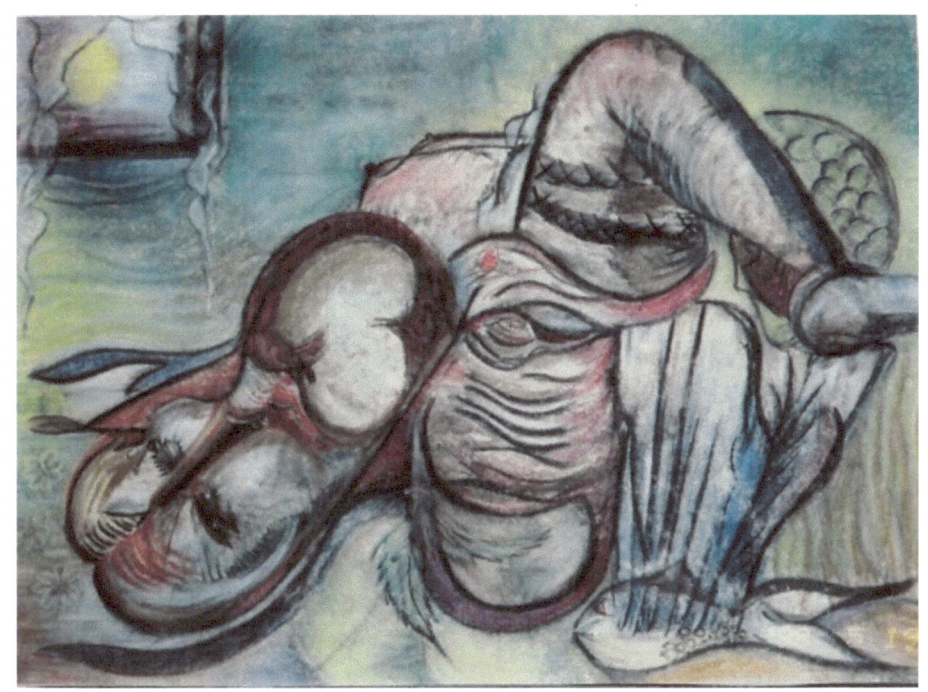

Face Me
Devorah Ticha
20"x26"
Pastel on paper

Do you hear those words I utter, late into the night?

Erin Foggoa

Imagineer
I paint and draw...
sing badly but loudly...
play roller derby...
love my baby girl with all of my heart...
spend waaay too much time on my computer...
use art as a way to get out of my head...
am constantly, irritatingly, thinking about my next art project...
print funny tshirts in my basement, and I love it...
love where I live and live where I love...
am grateful that I am an artist every.single.day...
live life according to Dr. Seuss.

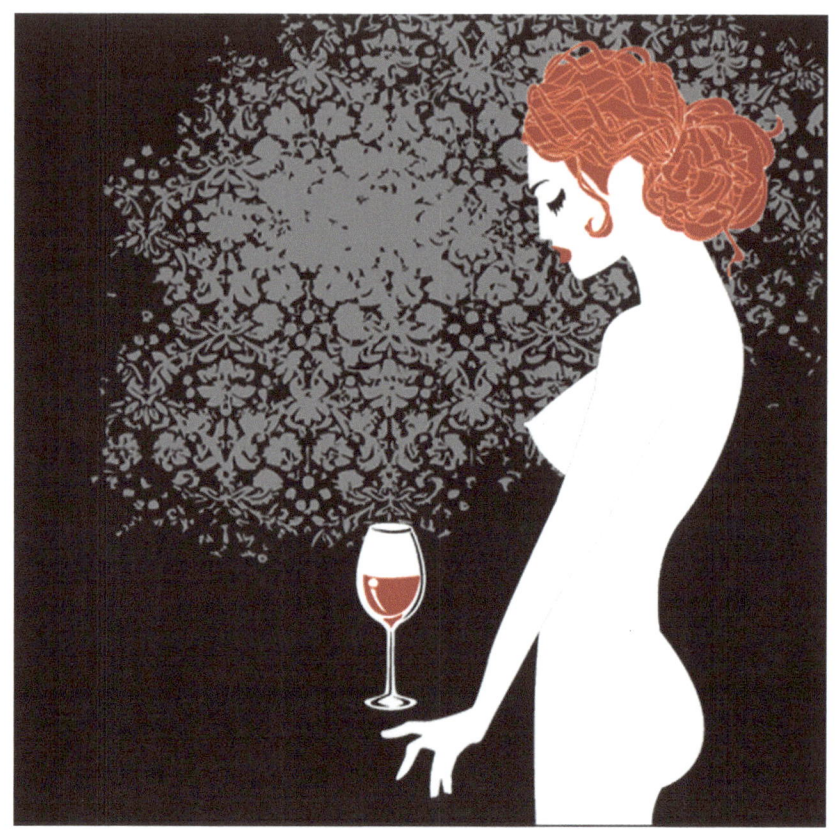

Redhead on the Edge
Erin Foggoa
36"x36"
Digital Illustration on Canvas

As the day had donned its jacket, the girl had removed hers.
Will she venture into night untold, or stay home alone again?

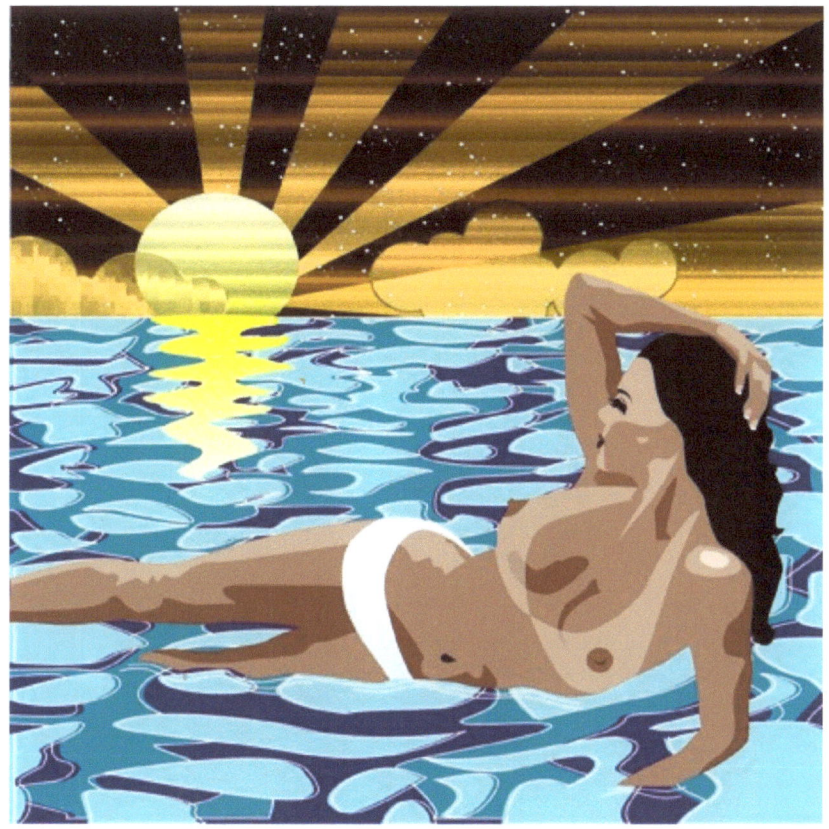

Siren of the High Seas
Erin Foggoa
36"x36"
Digital Illustration on Canvas

When pirates sailed the seven seas
And lost light, and time and season
They'd throw themselves in to the briny deep
And women like this were the reason

Gail Marie Kern

Gail Marie Kern lives in St. Paul Minnesota with her husband, several pets and too many plants. She enjoys paint and drawing comics.

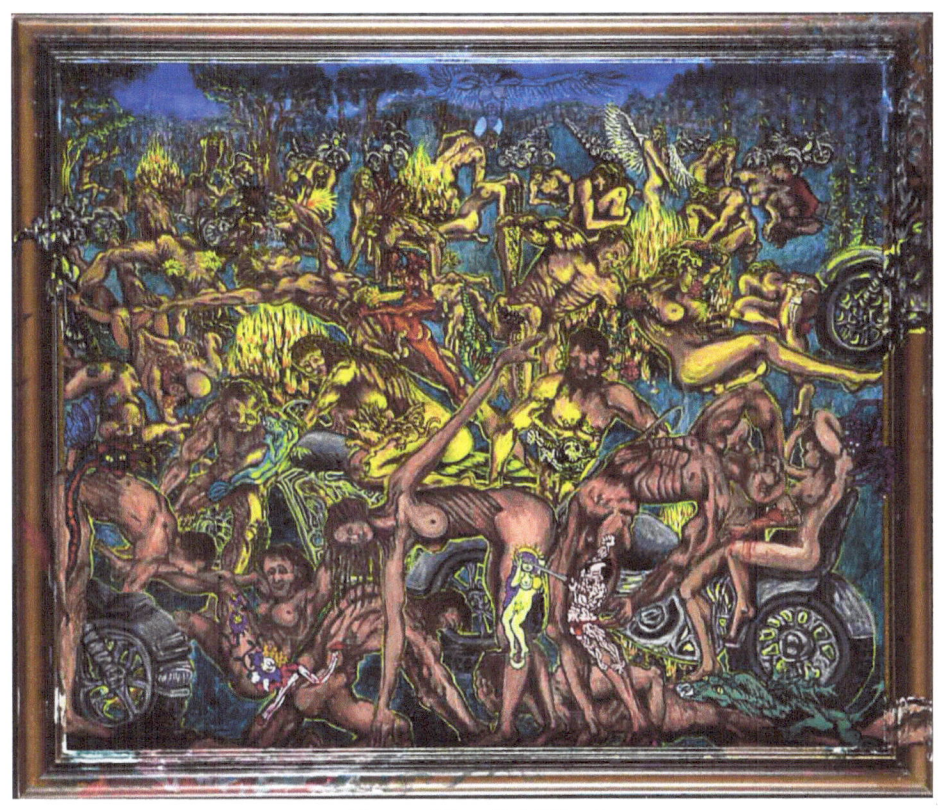

Choose Your Ink Wisely
Gail Marie Kern
25"x29"
Acrylic on masonite and wood frame

"Choose Your Ink Wisely" is about the struggle of the human soul. The tattoos or cartoon-like characters represent consequences to choices that the human figures have made. Some of the figures experience torment while others experience ecstasy. It is left up to the viewer to decide which. Each figure is on the brink of either heaven or hell. The scene suggests a motorcycle rally but is symbolic of any environment in which decadent behavior can be found.

Gary Mitchell

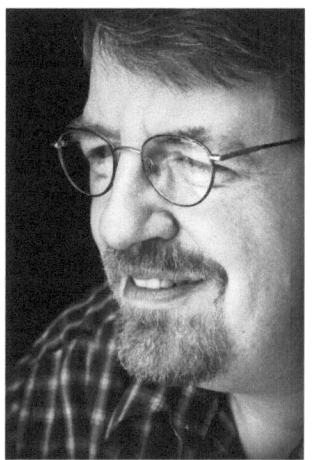

Gary Mitchell has been a photographer most of his life, and in 2006 turned his attention to artistic nude and erotic photography. He works in a classic style, preferring monochrome for most pieces, to better concentrate the viewer's attention on the form, gesture, strength and grace of his subjects. He lives in Dayton, Ohio, USA and runs a small advertising business.

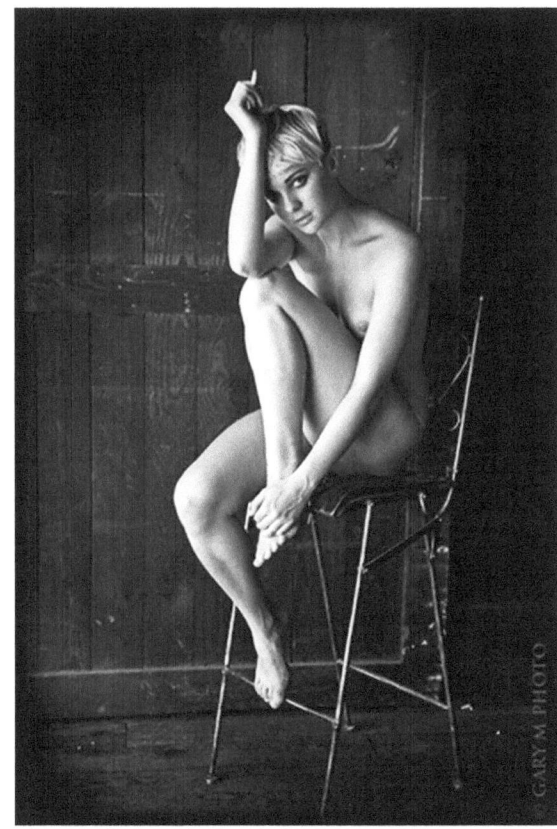

Chebo
Gary Mitchell
20"x16"
Photograph

A moment of reflection and relaxation with the
traditional cigarette.

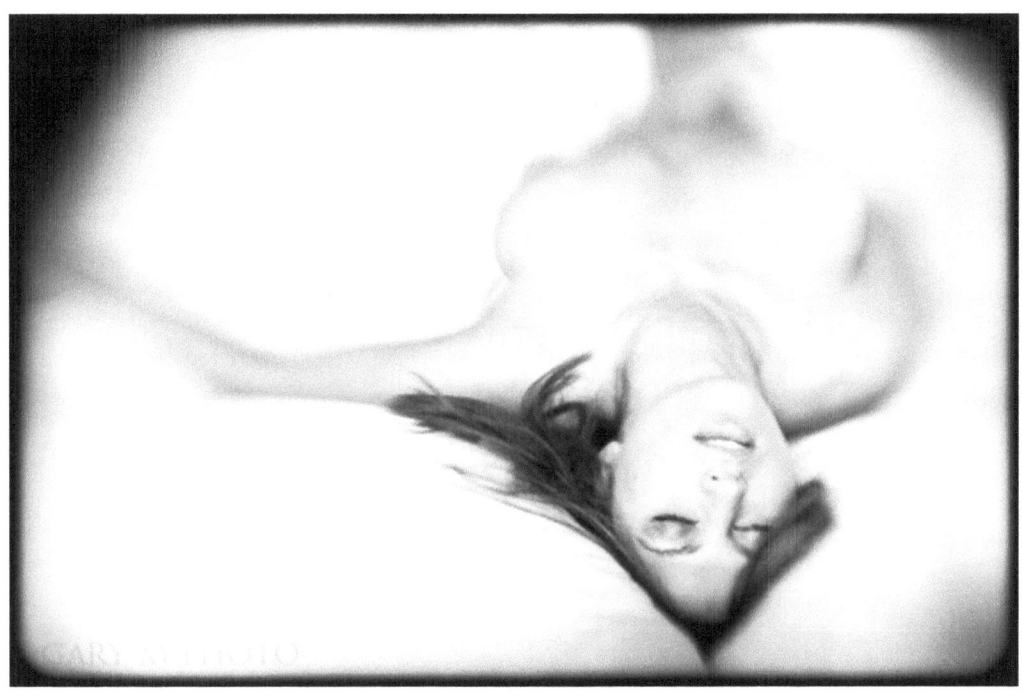

Soft Touch
Gary Mitchell
16"x20"
Photograph

A simple expression of private intimacy, the mind running free with thoughts of a distant loved one. The in-camera lens effect echoes the softness of a dream.

Greg Riley

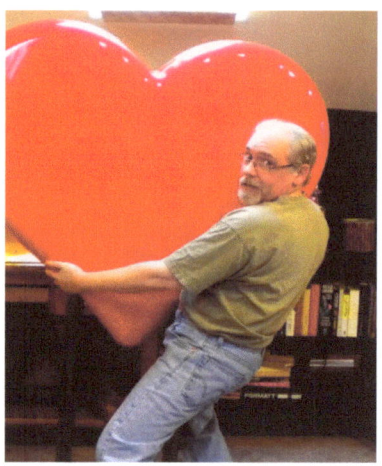

I have been an artist as long as I can remember. I am currently a mural painter by trade, but have worked as an illustrator, fine artist, sculptor, graphic artist, and portrait painter. I have been earning a living as an artist for 25 years and I am always ready to tackle the next project that comes into my studio. I studied at Joliet Junior College, American Academy of Art in Chicago, and at the Palette and Chisel Academy in Chicago.

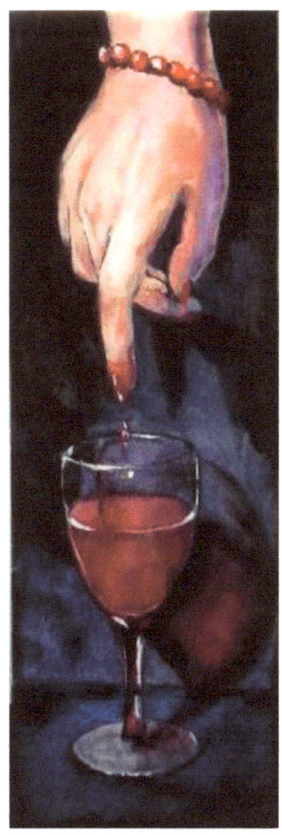

Nightcap
Greg Riley
12"x4"
Acrylic on canvas

Something sensual without being overtly sexual,
suggestive but not explicit, to create an open narrative
in the painting that encourages the viewer
to imagine their own story.

Jaine Buse

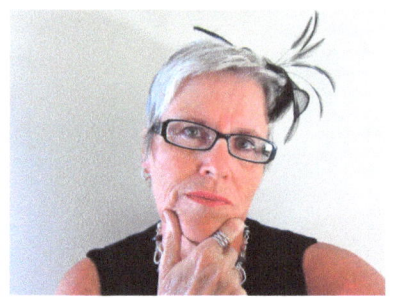

Painting from the inside out and feeling the intention is the focus for my creativity. The past 3 years in Kelowna has further allowed me to learn, observe and create images inspired from my surroundings and from the people I meet.

My "ART JOURNEY" is about paying attention to my purpose and passion and expressing it as I create. Art demands that I be true to myself and keep the fire from within lit.

I love Spontaneous Process Painting that involves layers, colors, depth, use of collage, mediums and piece of nature (tree bark, bee hives, grass, sheep's wool) imbedded in the layers.

My work is inspired from my travels in North and South America, Australia, New Zealand, China, Asia, Japan and Europe.

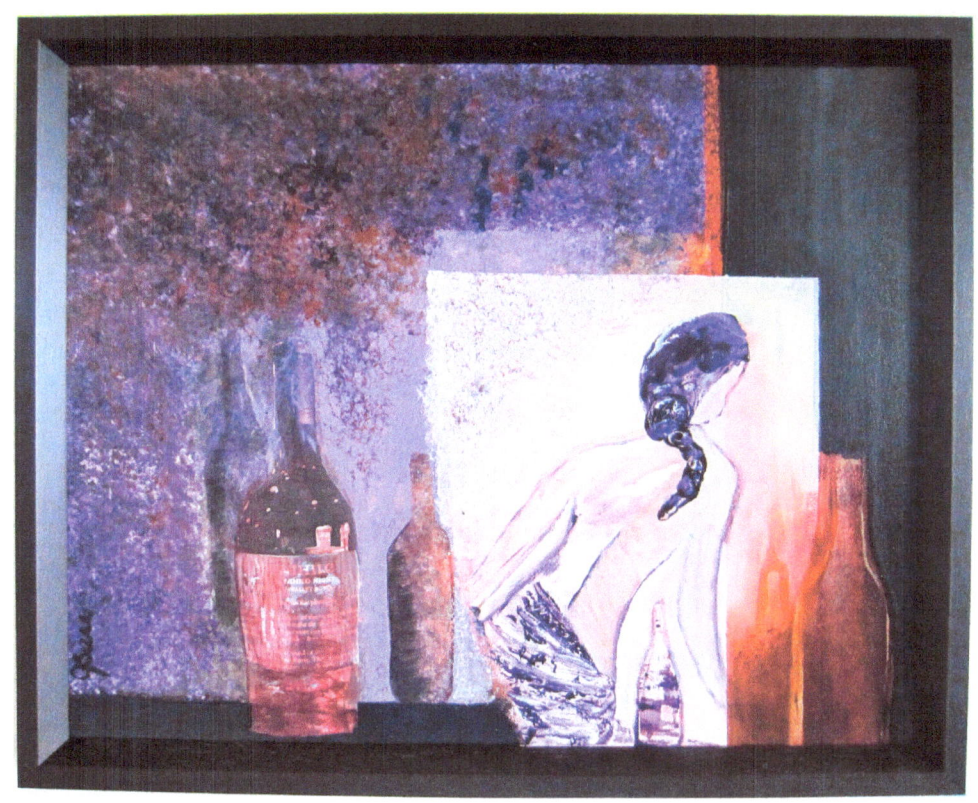

Window Dressing
Jaine Buse
32"x24"
Acrylic and Collage

Same time, every, evening: I know he is watching!!

Jennifer Burrows

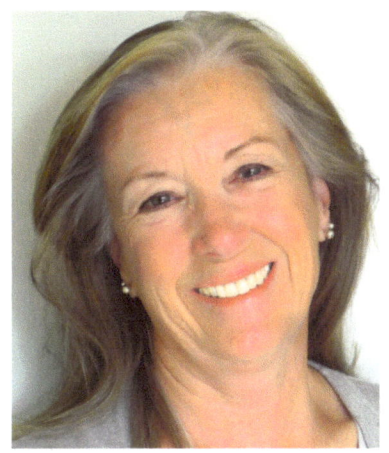

In 1978 I visited my first Robert Genn exhibit and realized painting would become my passion....
Eventually! I waited many years to complete my career as an educator which included teaching
grade 2-7 curriculum art. Now that I'm ecstatically retired I continue to learn from other artists
and from the land. The Okanagan landscape that I know and love teaches me to interpret what I
see, and to paint with the wonder and freedom I feel when hiking in the forest.

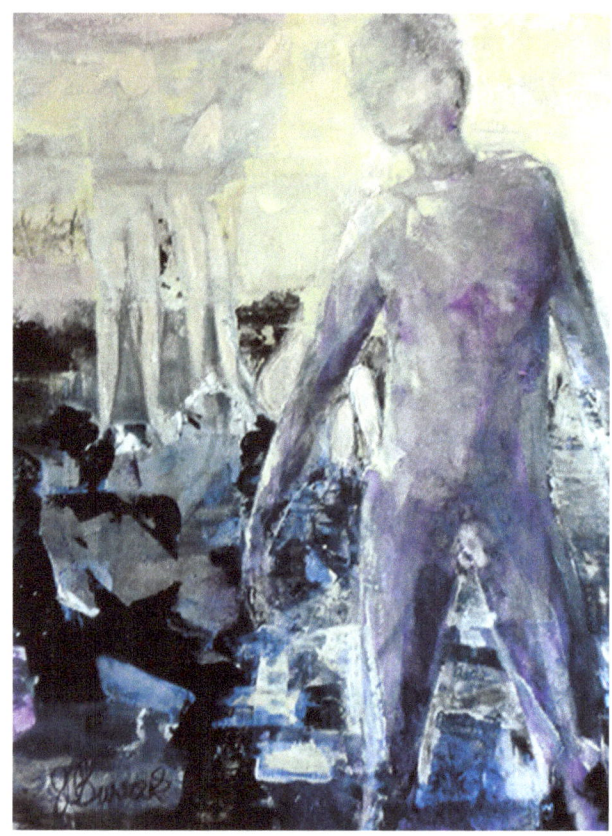

Twilight Exposure
Jennifer Burrows
24"x18"
Acrylic on canvas

Nightfall bares the soul ....daring us ...
what will happen if we listen.

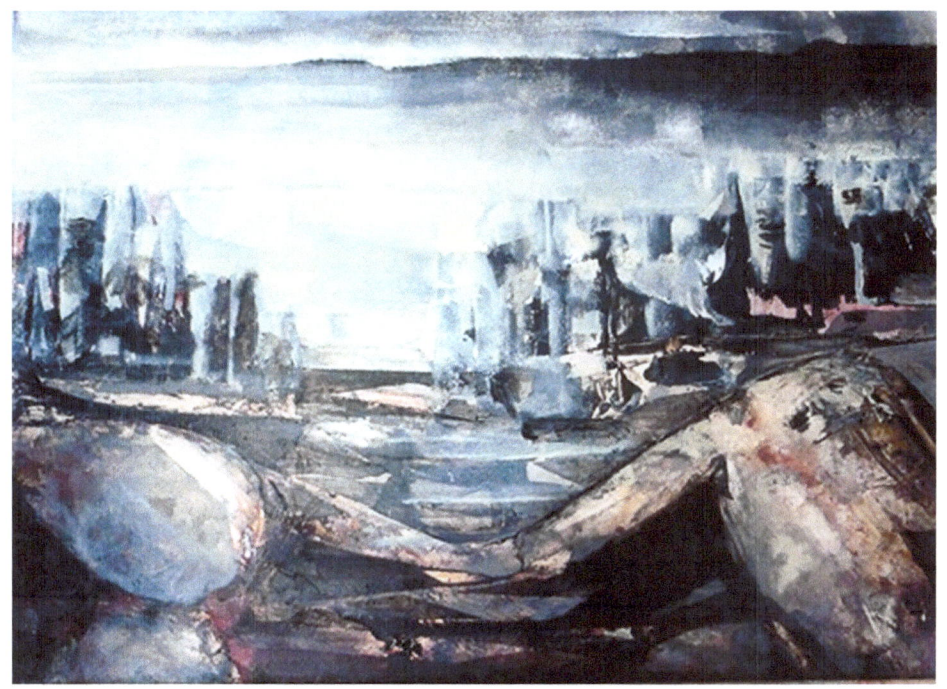

Seducing Nightfall
Jennifer Burrows
18"x24"
Acrylic and charcoal on canvas

Earth lies naked...waiting, wanting... to merge with Night.

Jim Britton

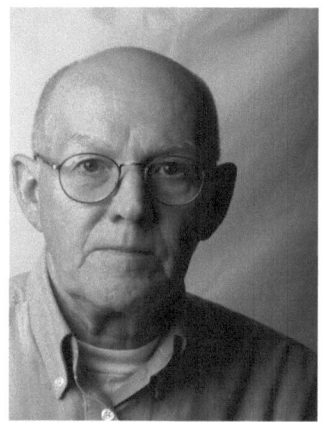

Jim Britton started his photography career at the age of four or five. His uncle, an amateur photographer, took Jim into his darkroom and taught him to make four by five and eight by ten prints. Jim bought his first camera when he was eight years old. His father encouraged him to purchase his own camera instead of constantly borrowing Dad's. In high school and college he photographed events for the school newspaper. One of Jim's classmates asked him to photograph their upcoming wedding and offered to pay Jim to do the job. Jim had found a career where people would pay him to do what he loved to do. Jim is now retired but still maintains his studio and darkroom.

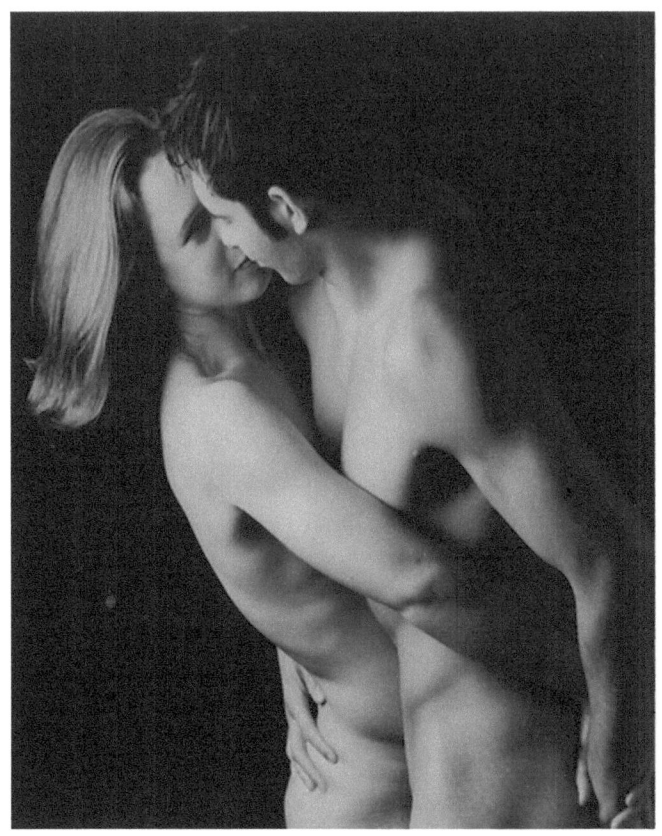

The Lovers
Jim Britton
Silver Emulsion Print from film

At the edge of night the lovers dance to the music that
only they can hear.
We see their dance but we can only imagine their music.

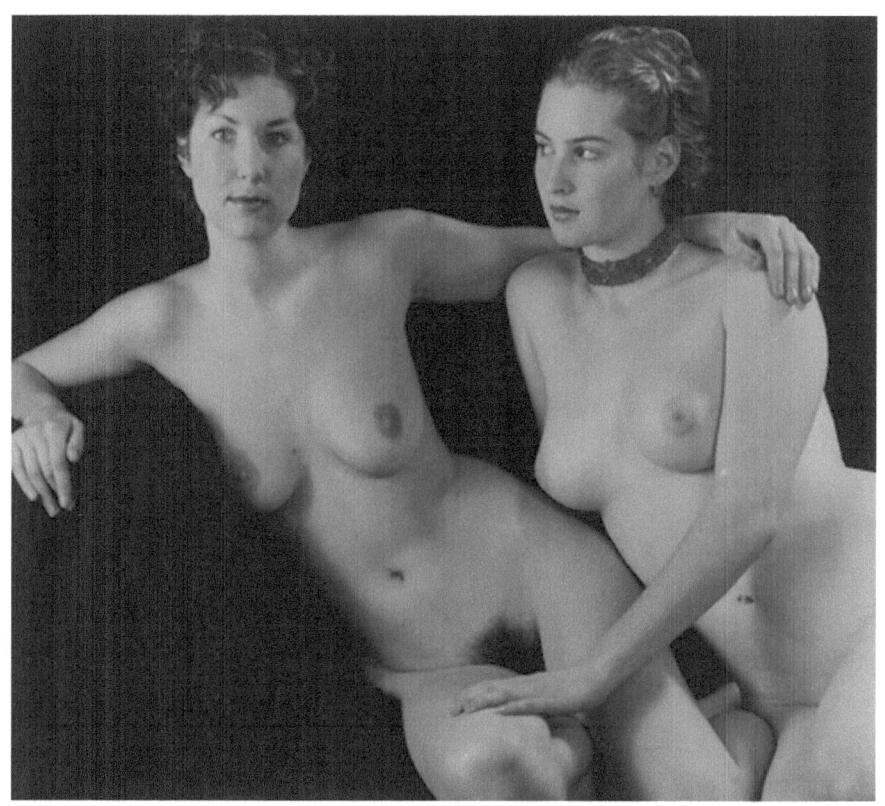

Friends
Jim Britton
Silver Emulsion Print from film

At the edge of night the friends are sitting together.
One glances lovingly at the other.
The other stares out at the viewer challenging the viewer's right to intrude.

Jim Duvall

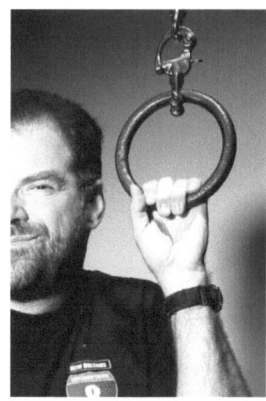

Jim Duvall began his career as an erotic photographer in the early days of the World Wide Web taking pictures for phone sex workers. He soon began janesguide.com along with his former partner Jane Duvall. Along with shooting for this company he has shot images for several other Web endeavors including bondage.com. His art has been shown at the Seattle Erotic Art Festival and many other erotic art festivals around North America. He helped start The Betty Pages, an LGBT magazine serving Whatcom and Skagit counties and was a writer and photographer for the magazine for 5 years.

As a sexuality activist Mr. Duvall has volunteered for many organizations over the years. He is a founder and former President of the Board of Directors of the Center for Sex Positive Culture (nee Wetspot). He founded the Seattle Erotic Art Festival. He is a past President and Board member of the National Coalition for Sexual Freedom.

Jim Duvall teaches on a variety of topics from erotic photography to rope bondage at events and for groups all over North America. His teaching style ranges from very hands on technique classes to demonstrations and entire class hypnosis or guided meditation.

Currently he works as a fine art photographer and practices hypnotherapy in Seattle WA.

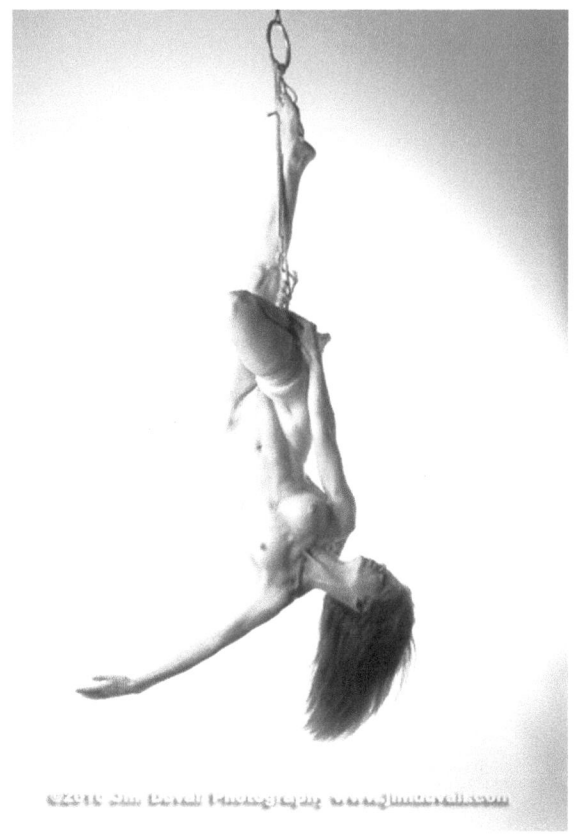

2010-2614
Jim Duvall
12"x18" framed 18"x 24"
Digital Photograph limited edition of 10 (2/10)

Bondage is really freedom, anything that constrains us
also gives us power and freedom.
Just as gravity allows us to walk the constraints here allow us to fly.

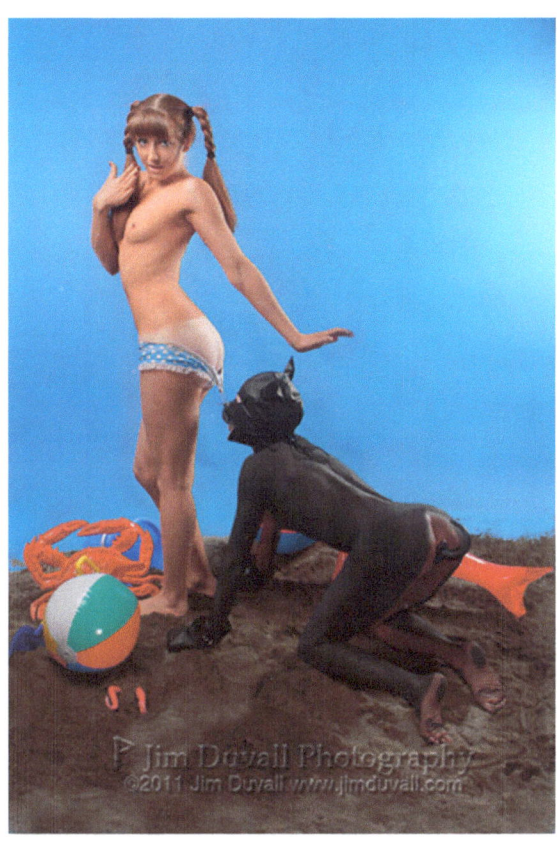

Title 2011-5076
Jim Duvall
12"x18" framed 18"x24"
Digital Photograph limited edition of 10 number 1 of 10

Images of old innocence since purged by a new puritanism.
This images takes back the edge of pinup art and revitalizes
nostalgia for innocence and sexuality in our society.

Johann Wessels

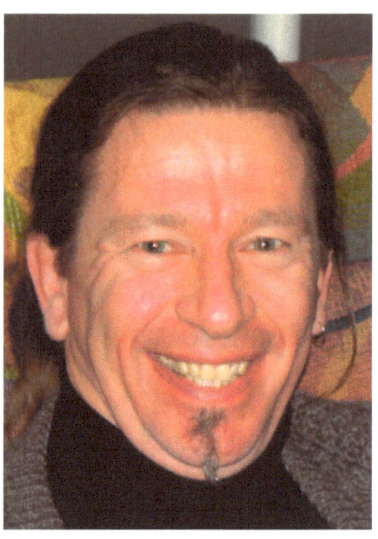

Born in South Africa, immigrated to Canada a decade ago. Worked in the film and TV industry for some time before going back to his own work and vision. Has a degree in Fine Arts, ex- university professor. Saskatchewan AAs Board Grant recipient in 2010. Johann lives in Penticton, BC.

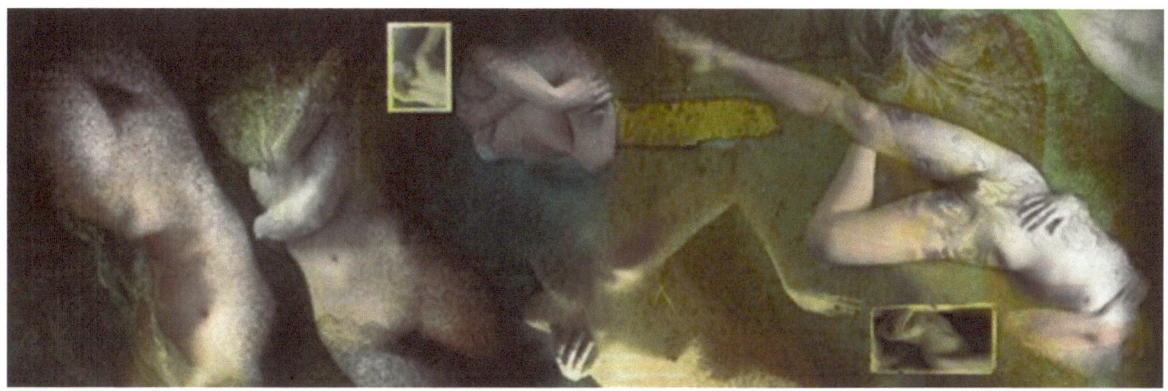

Green Nude
Johann Wessels
40"x13"
Digital and traditional painting

At twilight in the semi conscious, images swim and tantalize.

John Schnurrenberger

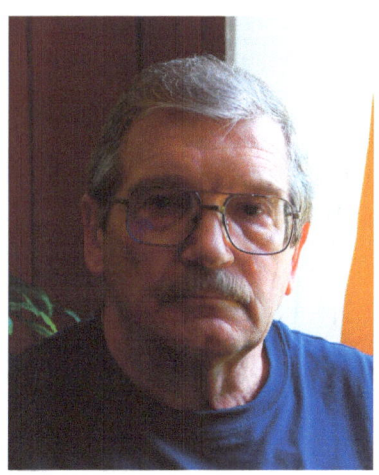

Born in Switzerland in 1941, both my wife Antje and I came to Canada in 1965 to live our dream.

In 1974 I began a lengthy and rewarding career as a "Western" Painter.
After many sell-out Shows, numerous limited - & open edition Prints & Posters, I am now mostly doing "Commission" work.

In the last 2 years I have concentrated on capturing the beauty and mystique of the female figure in a series of Drawings & Paintings. Currently my work is available at Gallery 421 in Kelowna, B.C, as well as at Altitude Gallery in Okotoks, Alberta

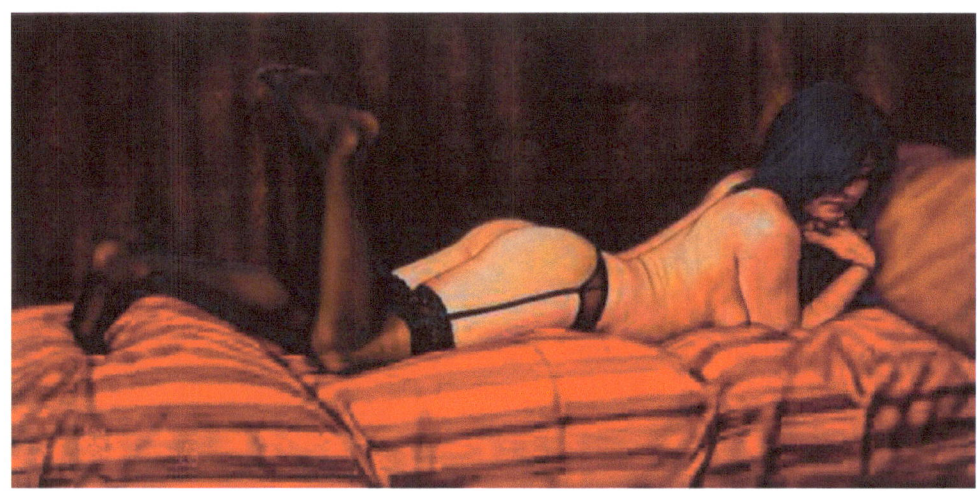

Intimate Thoughts
John Schnurrenberger
15"x30"
Oil on canvas

On the edge of evening a woman lays waiting.

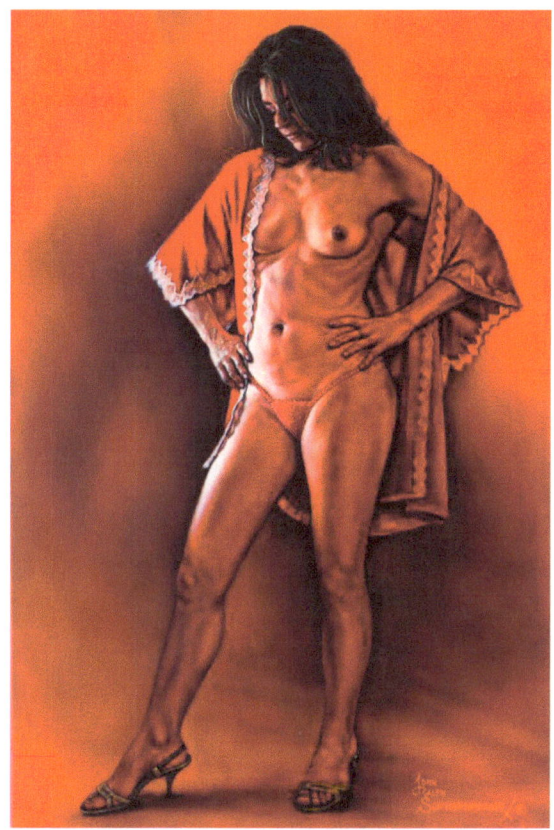

The Seductress
John Schnurrenberger
30"x20"
Oil on canvas

Sultry sunset caresses the clothes away and warms the skin.

Joyce Krenn

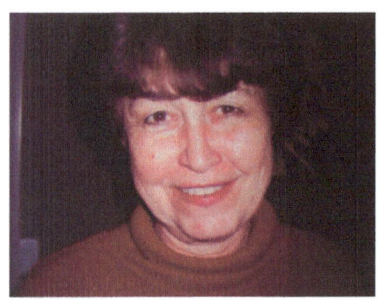

A Kelowna born artist, I mainly work on large oil on canvas, usually flowers. I do commissions and sell at Okanagan craft sales. Experimenting with more abstract and mixed media lately.

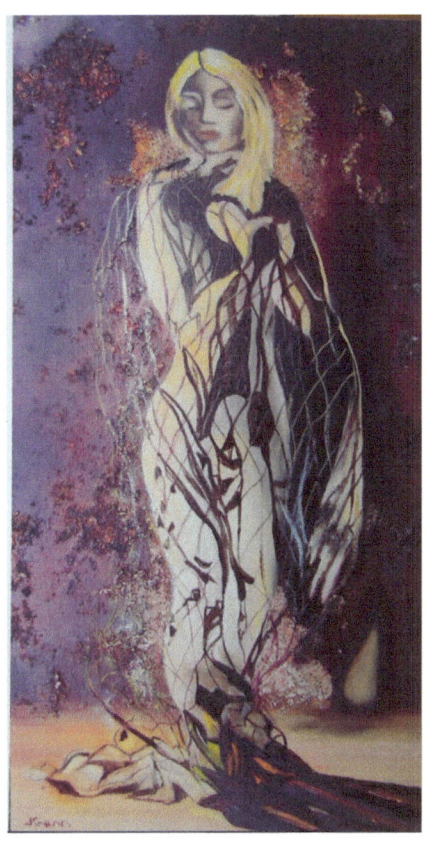

Lady of the Night
Joyce Krenn
24"x12"
Mixed Media

This Lady of the Night dared to appear in the glow of dusk. Her golden image created a seductive enchantment of desire for those viewing.
She allowed herself to be seen in this light and created an intense passion
that made for flirtatious venues taken to new heights
only to be experienced on the summer solstice.

Julia Trops

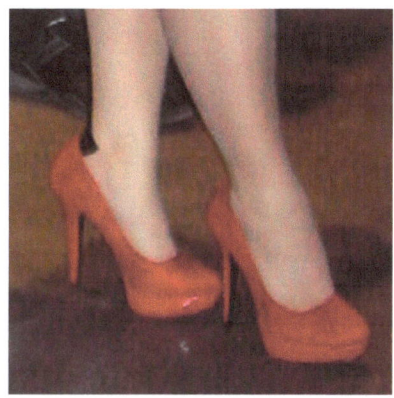

Julia Trops is an international multi-disciplinary artist having sold over 1100 artworks world-wide since 2004. Retaining the focus, work ethic and integrity from her 12 year career in the military, this decorated artist maintains a studio in the Rotary Centre for the Arts with three other local artists. Her work is vibrant, dramatic and expressive, and focuses on the feminine figure.

While other writers have selected her artwork numerous times for publishing, Julia is close to completing her fourth book. Julia is one of the original organizers of the Okanagan Erotic Art Show and has carried on the event on her own since 2009. Livessence Society for Figurative Artists and Models was born from Julia's life drawing sessions started in 2003 and won the 2010 Central Okanagan Community Group Arts Award.

Julia is represented in the Okanagan by Gallery Odin at Silver Star Ski Resort, at Creatio Ex Nihilo, and in the Rotary Centre for the Arts.

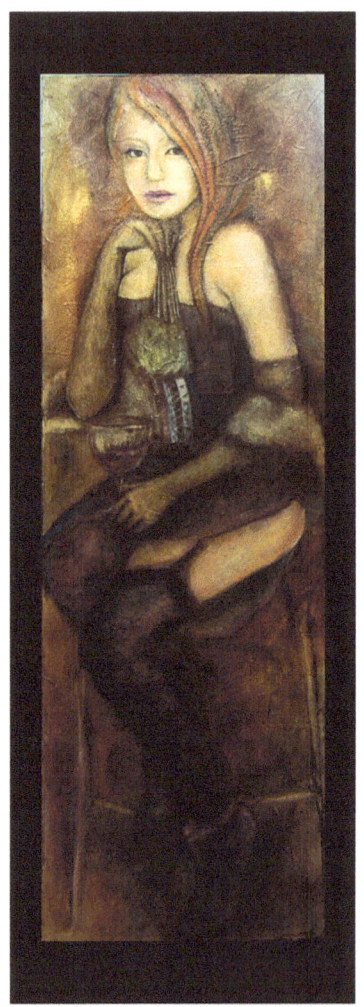

She's making plans
Julia Trops
36"x12"
Mixed Media

Tied up yet? If not already, you will be....

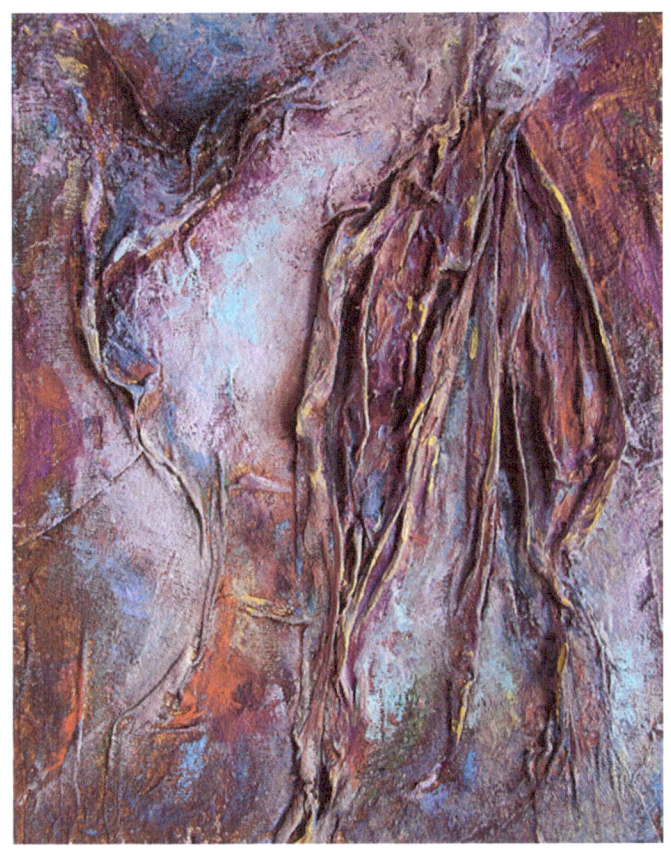

69
Julia Trops
14"x11"
Mixed media

Up close and personal.

Karen Rempel

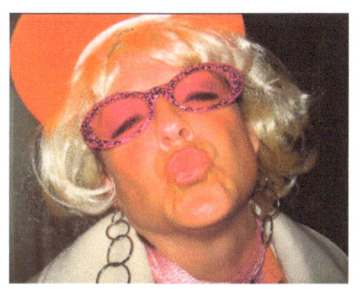

Karen (Kato) Rempel is an explorer of this
ecosystem – at this moment in time.
With a 20 year background in graphic and web
design, she has now ventured into the realm of painting erotic concepts,
creative landscapes and blurry nights of intriguing conversation...
She is exploring all aspects of herself, of her
creative expression and her inner being. With this, her art reflects different
moods, different creative mediums and different topics. Just different.

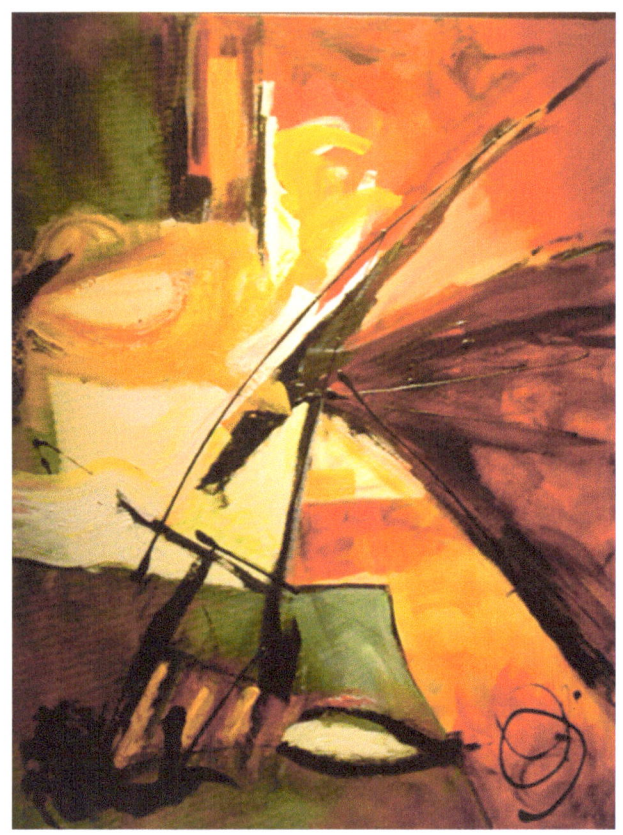

The Pain of Passion
Karen Rempel
40"x30"
Acrylic on canvas

Inspired by Adam Lambert's
Whataya Want from Me.

Play me like a violin
place your bow upon my strings
soft and gentle, to and fro
hold me tight, don't let me go.
Make our music
oh, so sweet
awakening feelings
that will grow
our love, together
so complete
as only, we can know.

Rhythm and rhyme
and harmony
this, together – pure symphony
not, a care in the world have we
as long as you are here with me...

So, Play me
like a violin
place your bow
upon my strings
soft and gentle, to and fro
hold me tight, don't let me go

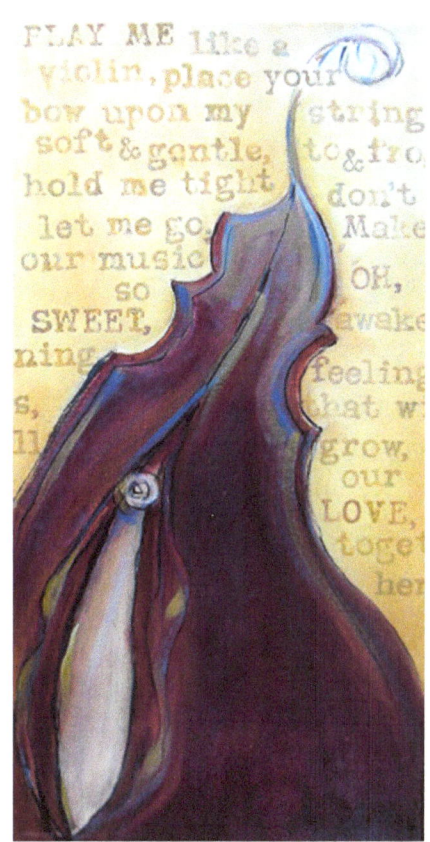

Play Me
Karen Rempel
36"x12"
Acrylic on canvas

Karen Rudolph

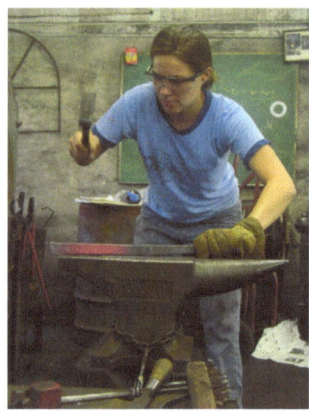

After graduating from Warren Wilson College in 2002, Ms. Rudolph became the resident blacksmith at the John C. Campbell Folk School in Western North Carolina. She spent a number of years studying under the watchful eye of master blacksmiths and coordinating the year round educational blacksmith shop.

Ms. Rudolph now lives in Chattanooga, Tennessee, and spends her days juggling the responsibilities of a much too large garden, a blacksmith studio, and her day job at a local Foundation which supports the regions arts and artist.

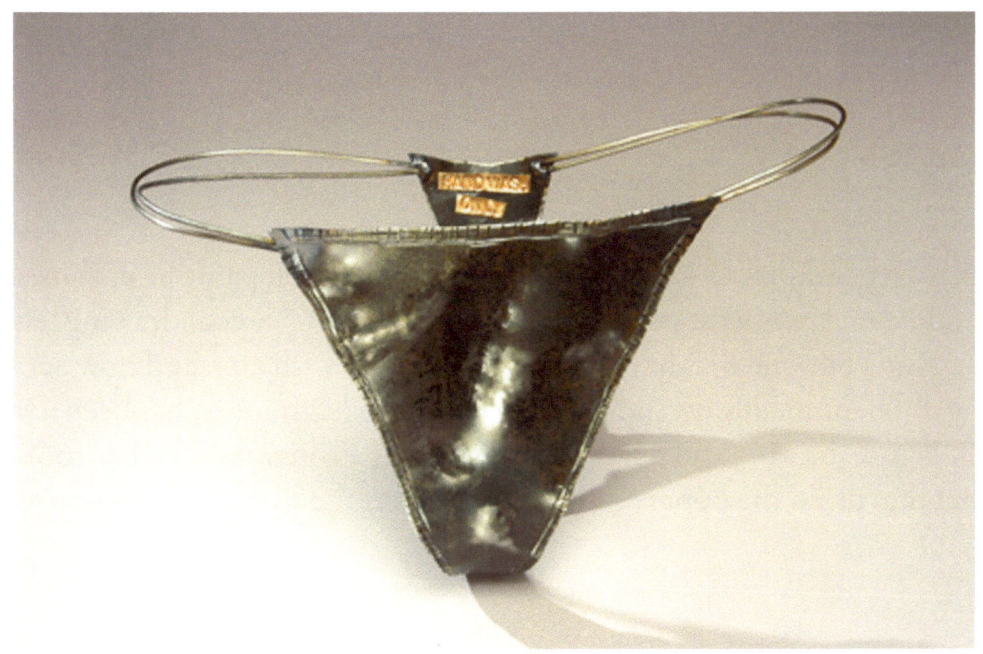

Iron Clad
Karen Rudolph
Iron and Copper

Iron Clad : dark and cool : as the edge of the night sky.

Karla Warkotsch

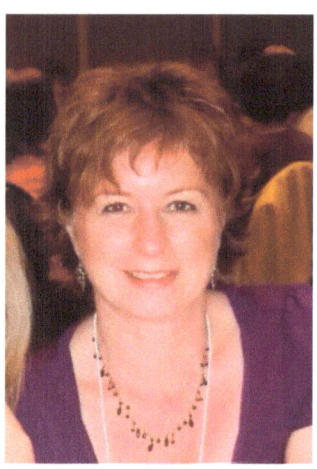

From the time of young childhood, Karla Warkotsch joined her oil painting enthusiast parents to live model art classes with pencil and paper in hand. Charcoal drawing has always been a passion for Karla but one that has shared the spotlight with clay, and now acrylics and pastels. Exploring different mediums, and pushing herself to learn more, has been a journey of self expression. Figure drawing and painting feeds Karla's strong ties with her roots and supports her belief that given the opportunity, everyone has the spark of creativity to nurture our souls.

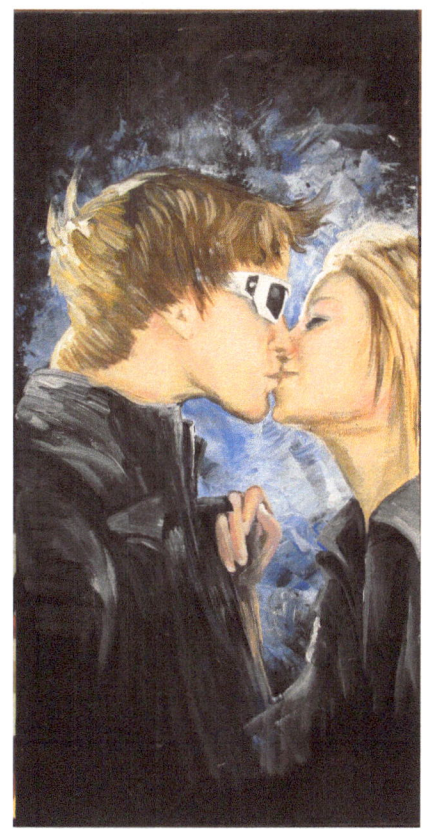

First Kiss
Karla Warkotsch
24"x12"
Acrylic on canvas

Night seduction enfolds young
lovers into dreams of passion and
promises of love. The first kiss; soft,
warm, exciting..........

Kendi Clearwater

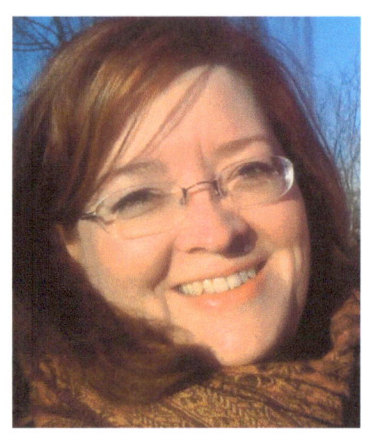

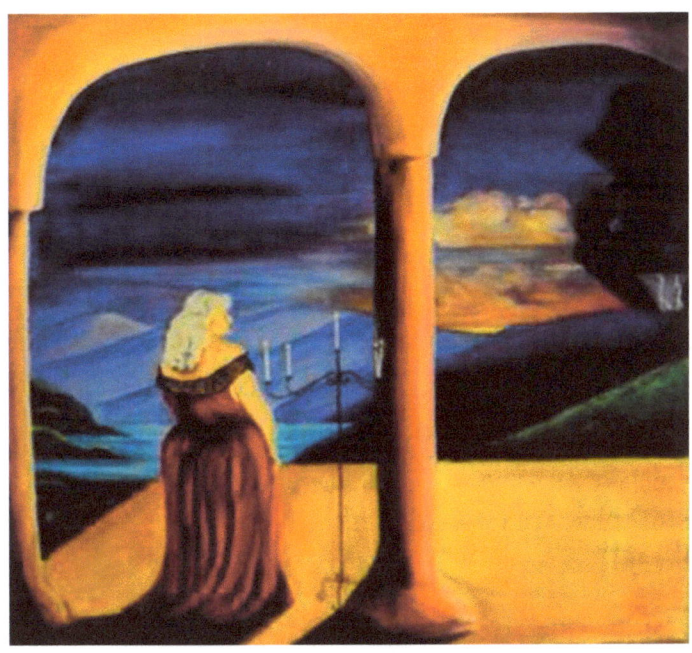

"She Walks in Beauty Like the Night
Kendi Clearwater
36"x36"
Acrylic painting on Canvas

"She Walks in Beauty Like the Night" is meant to capture the sensuous beauty and eroticism of women at all stages of their life. The lady in the painting faces an impending storm, faces the sunset, and faces the approaching night over the Okanagan landscape with grace, and beauty. Unafraid of who she is, she wears a gown of the deepest red showing off her shoulders letting the night breeze cool her skin, electricity from the approaching thunderstorm filling the air. Mystery and possibility are suggested, contrasts make the viewer slightly on edge..an older woman who hints at her sexuality, is she waiting for a lover? Can the viewer accept that older women are sexy and sexual? The night and the landscape are overshadowed by the impending storm, the sense of space is contrasted with the intimacy of the moment. These are the elements that are meant to invite the viewer to explore the relationship between eroticism and death.. between ourselves and the celebration that is life and between our fears and the inevitability of our own death.

"Thus mellow'd to that tender light
Which Heaven to gaudy day denies"-   from She Walks in Beauty Like the Night by Lord Byron

Koreena Lane

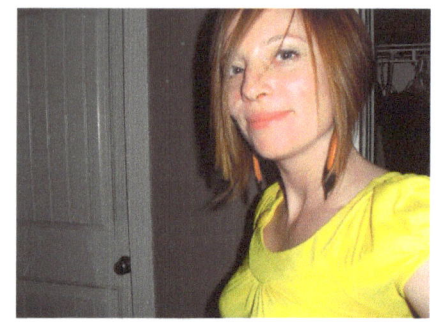

Being small town raised and always poor has given me the ability to get creative with what I consider "art supplies". Using anything from sticks and corn silk to build fairies to making paint brushes with my hair allows for a wonderful array of combinations to come to life. While I have no formal training past high school, I have always been possessed by the need to create and feel most often that I am merely a conduit rather than an artist. I always try to bring a little bit of cheekiness and fun to my art and life.

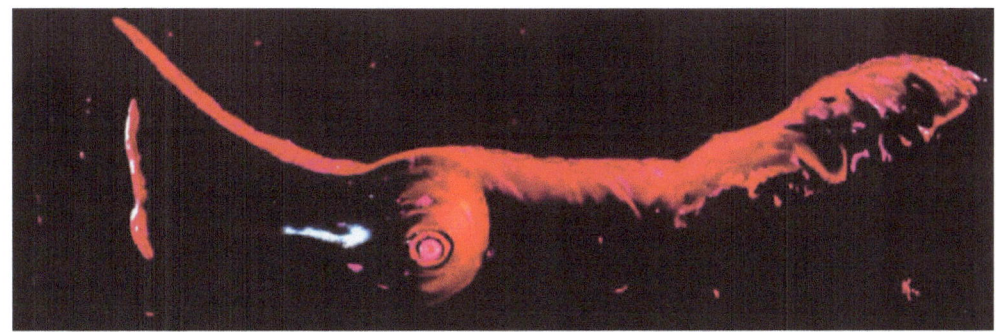

Tune in Tokyo
Koreena Lane
Functional Radio

Tweaked titties torment the timid though the tweeters tame the tempted.

Laura F. Klopp

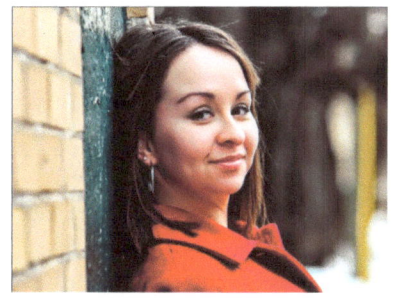

Laura is a young artist residing in Indianapolis, Indiana (USA) who dreams of making it in a big city one day. She enjoys a good fine-dining restaurant, philosophy, writing poetry, thunderstorms, classical music, and her beloved rescue cat, Tiaga. Though she went to school for fine art, she spends her days working at an animal hospital and her nights drawing with her favorite medium – colored pencil. She briefly spent some time in Italy studying Renaissance art and fell in love with Caravaggio and the Old Masters all over again. Laura constantly strives for a dramatic light source in her work which is currently focusing on the human figure.

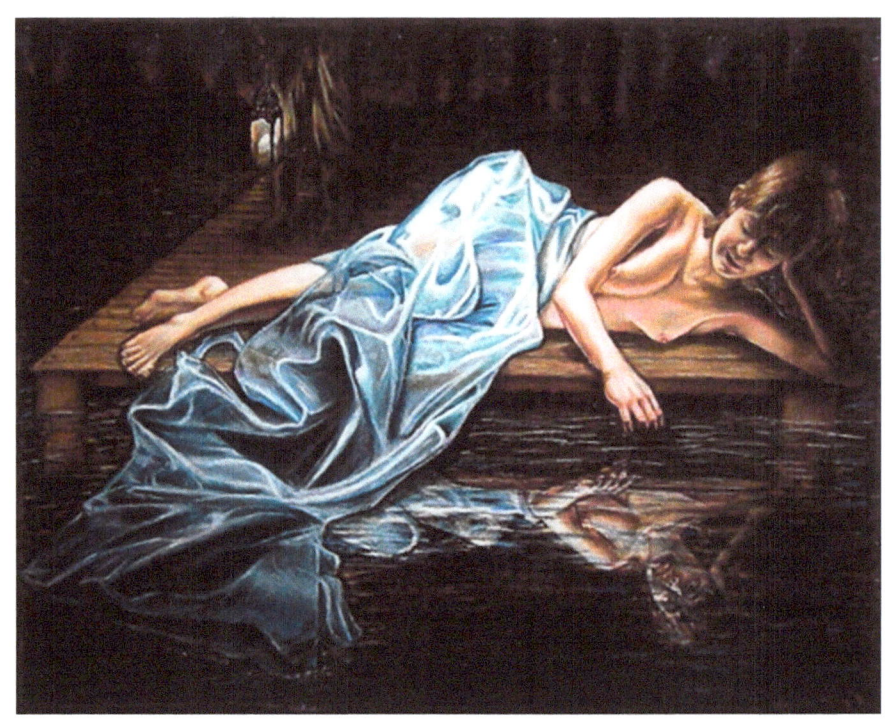

Summer Siren
Laura F Klopp
25"x29"
Colored pencil with pastel

Summer nights are intoxicating and the perfect chance to
explore your true self.

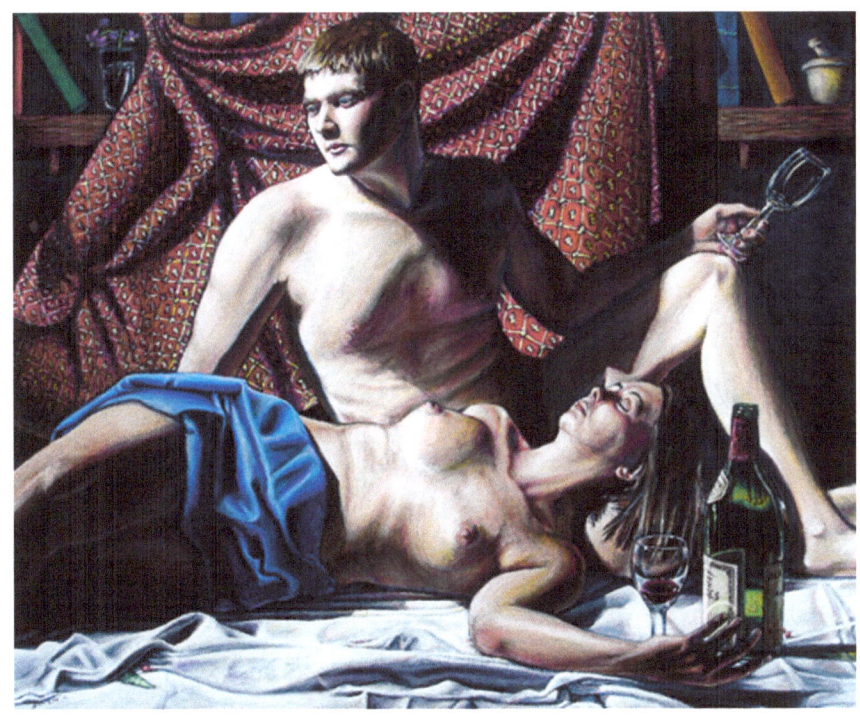

An Unfortunate Evening Affair
Laura F Klopp
28"x32"
Colored pencil with acrylic and pastel

Tonight, the air hangs thin and everyone gets a little more
than they bargained for.

Lauri Copeman

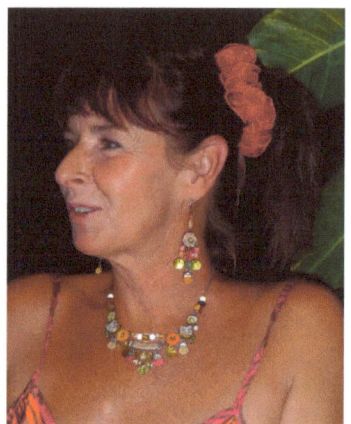

I am self-taught. Over twenty years my work has evolved into a style I call Emotional Realism. I paint portraits of people, places and things that mirror inner reality than outer. We are not a product of our environment. Our environment is a product of us.

My work hangs in private collections Mexico, Canada and the USA. Currently:
- Artist in residence at The Rotary Center for the Arts, Studio 113, in Kelowna BC
- Active Member of the Federation of Canadian Artists
- Member of Livessence Society of Figurative Artists and Models

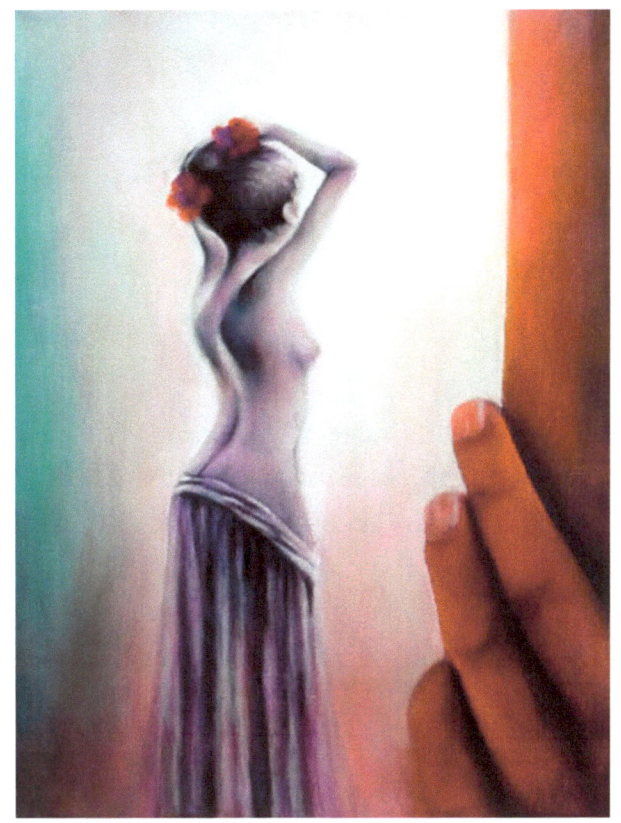

Cracking the door
Lauri Copeman
12"x9"
Oil on canvas

If you knew that I was watching,
would your heart pound as hard as mine?

Lesley Harris

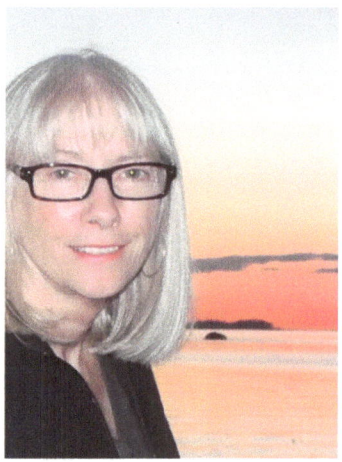

I am a Gabriola artist who dabbles in a wide variety of media. My main interest presently is pet and human acrylic portraits in a photo-realism style. For the last 7 years, however, I have also produced one-of-a kind beaded cuffs and costume jewellery. Although I've been pursuing various artistic outlets since the 1960s, the chance to live by the ocean in close proximity to wildlife is inspiring and a gift. I truly believe we are all artistic and that all we need is the encouragement and opportunity to step out of our own way and let it flow.

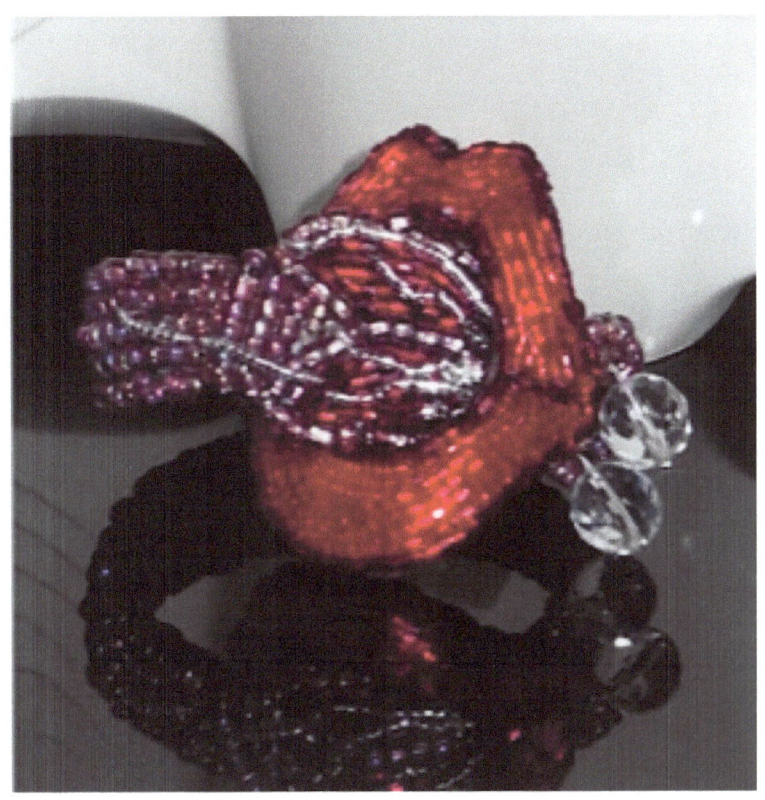

Hidden Depths
Lesley Harris
Beaded cuff, glass beads, Japanese delicas and deer skin

To me erotica is about the hidden or suggested. I love an inside joke or a secret shared by friends. The cuff appears to be a bejewelled bracelet for perhaps an evening event or, as has been suggested, a tribute to the Rolling Stones. The wrist band while appearing snake-like is in fact much naughtier.

Lisa Figueroa

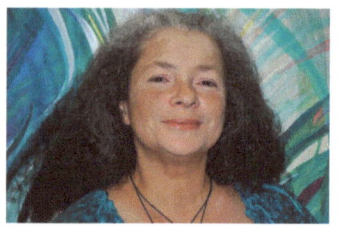

Lisa Figueroa is passionate about nudes. Lisa knew she was in the right place when she first entered a life drawing studio at 19. Lisa is tantalized by the human form and has spent a life time marveling at the beauty and capturing the nuances of: movement, emotion, mass, colour and drama of the nude. Lisa has always enjoyed a good story and finds a large part of the joy of creating Erotic Art is the magical possibilities of story line. Dreaming and speculating one's own story to any given piece of art is a large part of the joy of viewing Erotic Art. The enticing view has always been Lisa's goal.

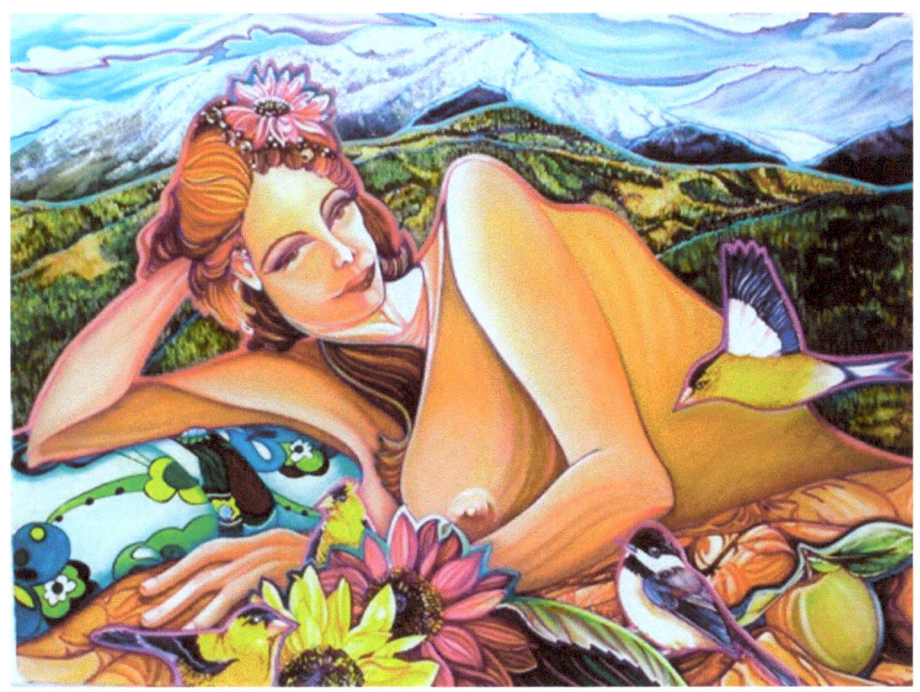

Harvest
Lisa Figueroa
Watermedia

On the Edge of Night, Harvest longs to seduce her Lover. As the sun sets over the frosty hills Harvest beckons her Lover to be nourished at her breast and to taste the fruits of her labour.

Lisolette Gilcrest

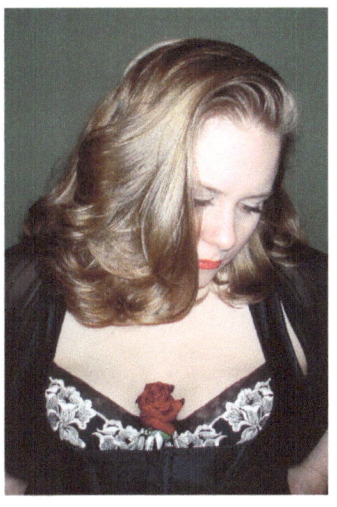

Featured in the permanent collection of the renowned Kinsey Institute's Special Art, Artifacts and Photography Collection, Lisolette Gilcrest is noted for her distinctly feminine and whimsical erotica that she says is focused less on "the deed" and more on the delicious intangibles. Lisolette is a two-time Erotic Signature Winner (2009 and 2010), has been featured by the Erotic Review, as well as published in four other books, and is the founder of the Society for Women in Erotic Art Today. Lisolette is represented by Streetwise Art.

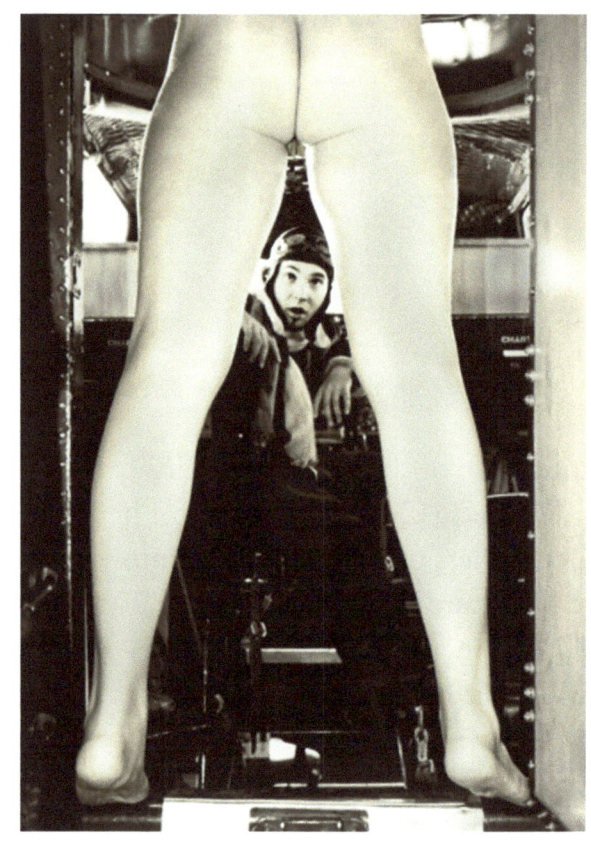

Cockpit
Lisolette Gilcrest
Limited Edition #7 of 27
Digital Photography

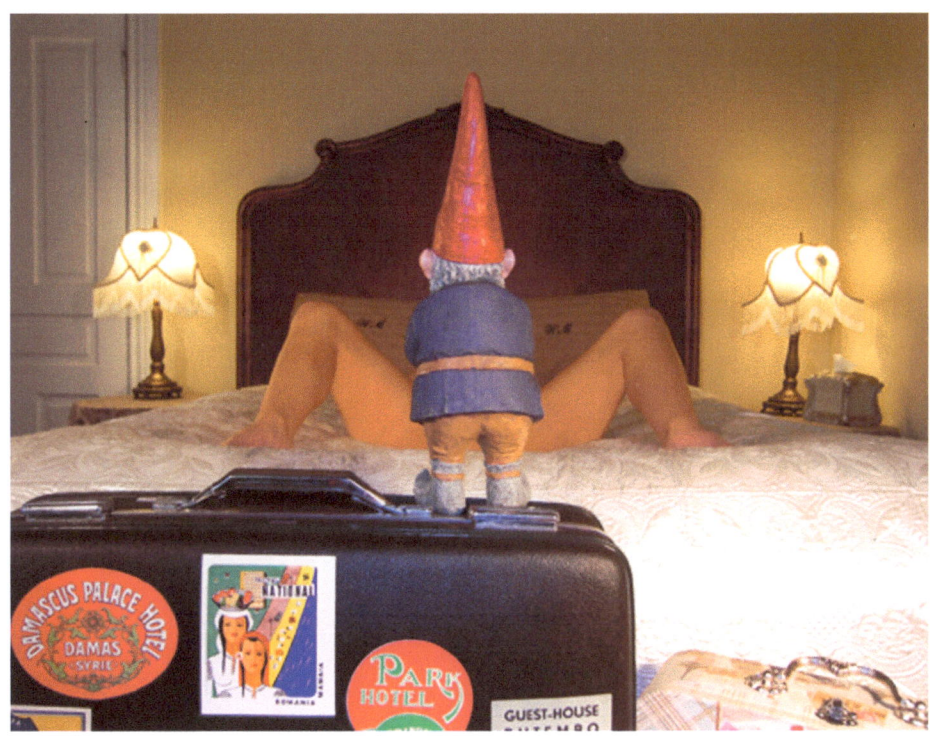

Gnome Liberation Front
Lisolette Gilcrest
Limited Edition #2 of 27
Digital Photography

Marissa Brown

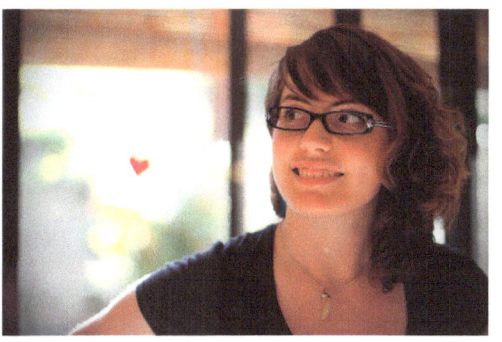

I am a 22 year-old queer artist originally from Vernon, BC. Power, sexuality, spirituality, and femininity interest me, and the more I can learn, try on, sample and taste, the better. A firm believer that all knowledge is worth having.

 I am a full-time 4th year BFA student and the Executive Coordinator of the Pride Resource Centre at UBC Okanagan.

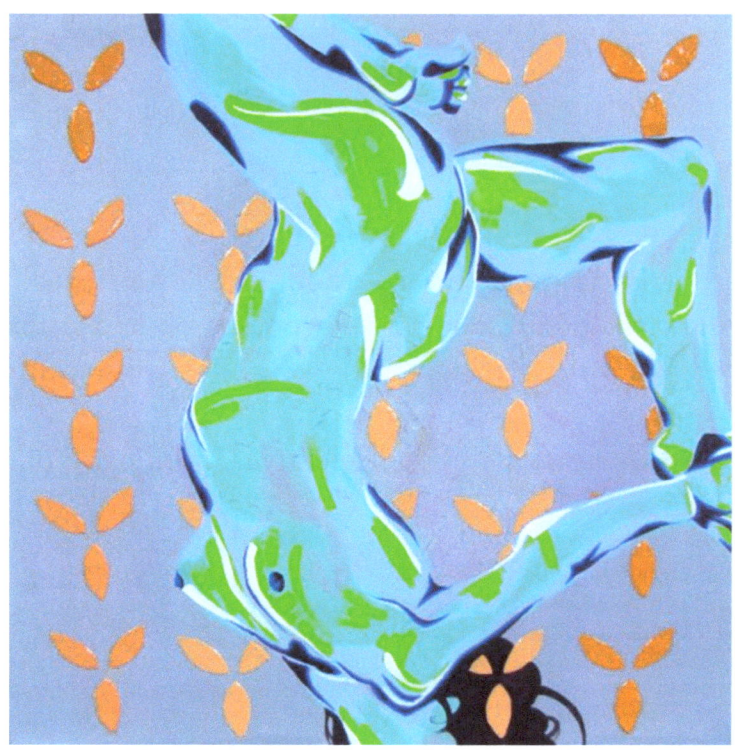

Suspension of Movement
Marissa Brown
42"x42"
Acrylic

Caught, in that indefinite universe between desire and satisfaction.

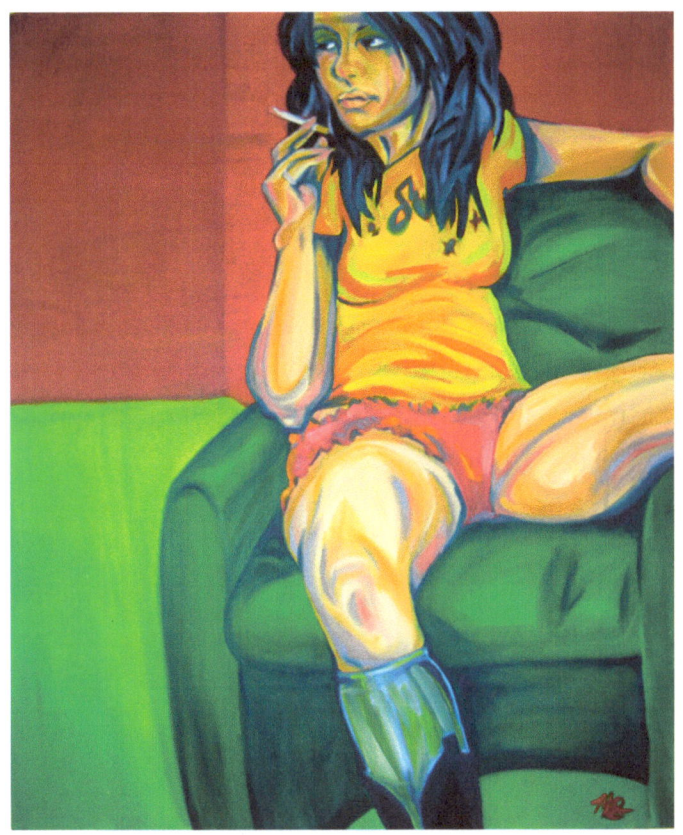

Princess
Marissa Brown
45"x55"
Oil

In the end, nothing is quite as sweet as a cigarette.

Patricia Feist

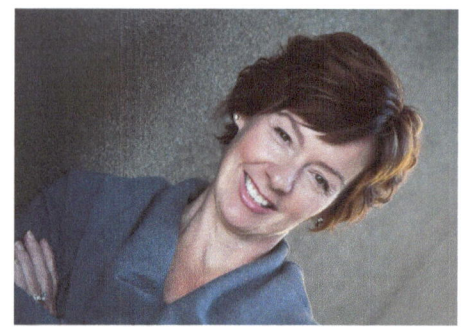

The tantalizing question, "what if ?" intrigues me and leads me to new adventures. With art, as with life, I don't seek perfection-simply the opportunity to challenge myself, to be daring and to do things many say shouldn't be done. We have each been given a precious gift. What we decide to do with that gift is what is important.

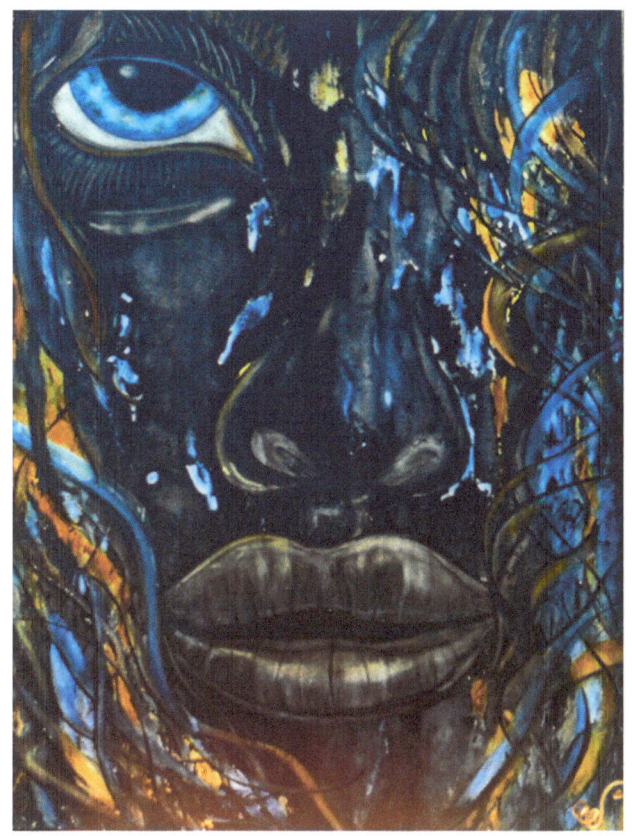

Entanglement
Patricia Feist
30"x40"
Acrylic

Primal Urges surface as the moon rises

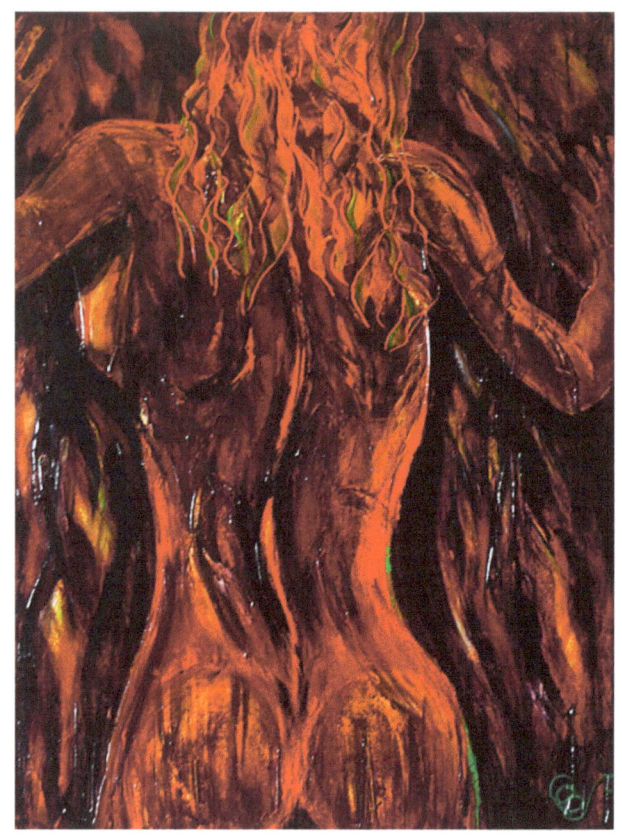

Heat
Patricia Feist
36"x48"
Acrylic

Surrender your inhibitions and embrace the passions ignited within

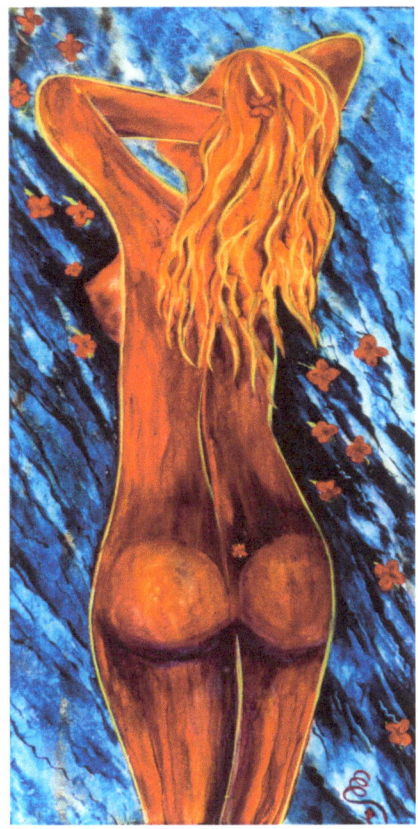

Free To Be
Patricia Feist
36"x18"
Acrylic

Sensing your approach, she smiles to herself and continues

Ronnie Olson

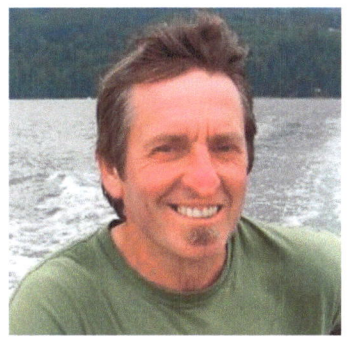

In 1990 I created the first high-definition, 3-D imaging system specifically for imaging living, breathing (unless otherwise occupied) human beings. The results were so compelling that I was given a licensing agreement by playboy enterprises to image Playmates and in the twenty years since I have had the extreme good fortune to have imaged more than a hundred women. I have been featured in erotic art venues throughout the world - my new web site (www. sexyholography.com) details my personal portfolio to include many commissioned Boudoir pieces. The comment I so often hear is "it's like they're right there behind the glass" and I never tire of it.

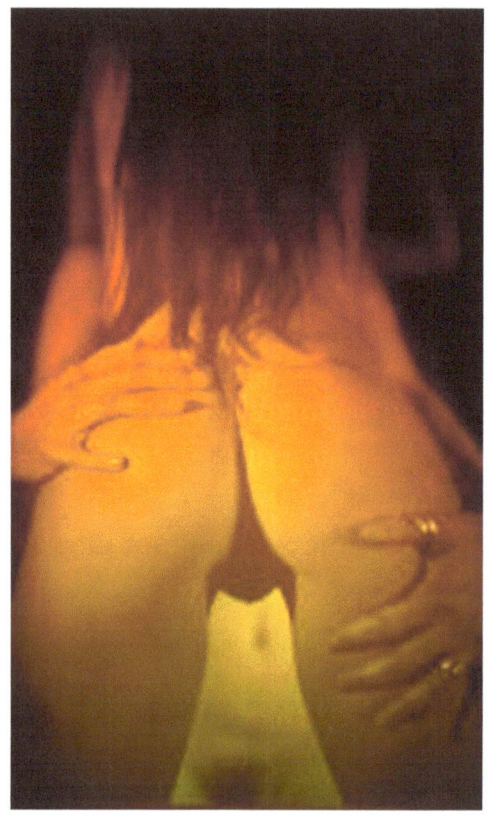

Cuddling
Ronnie Olson
22"x18"
Holography on Glass

My works are created to reflect the incredible detail of the human body and the sexuality it inspires.

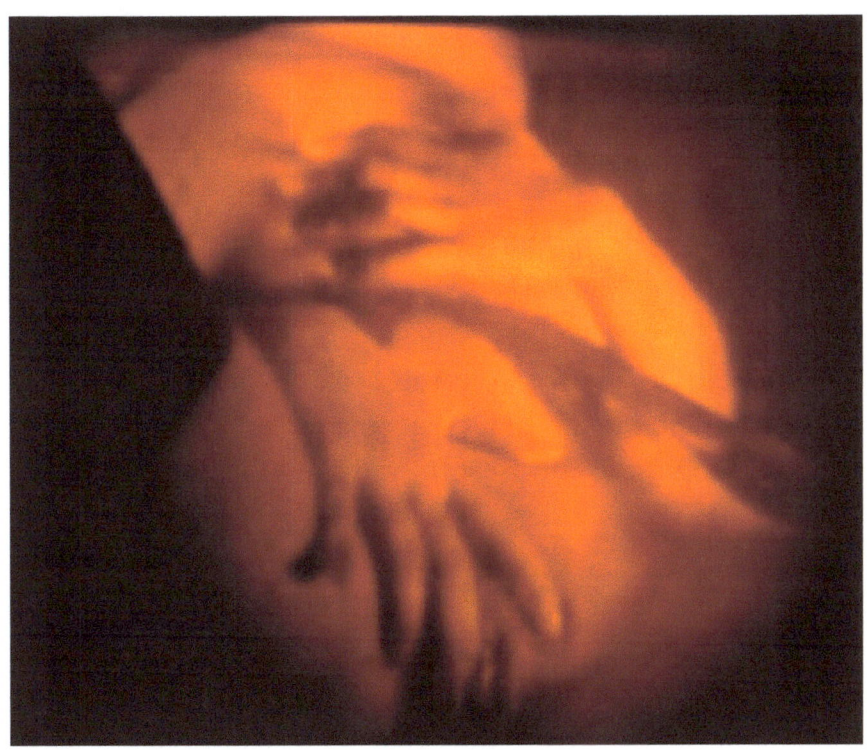

Sweet Lips
Ronnie Olson
19"x19"
Holography on Glass

I am most happy when my work results in viewers swallowing hard while questioning their perception of reality . and always when giving serious cause to smile.

Roxi Sim Hermsen

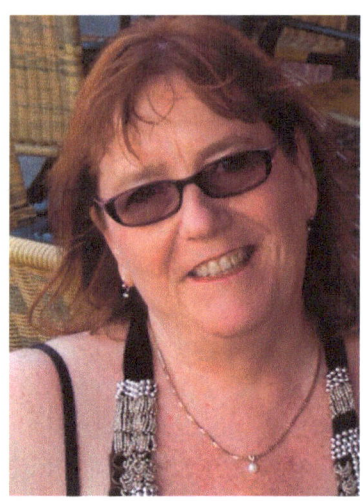

BEd FA Dip. FA Vernon based, Roxi started painting seriously in Grenada W. I., going through 200 ft. of canvas and a suitcase full of paint. Her paintings are inspired by bright Caribbean colours, textures, flora, fauna, people and culture. Oh, and a few (wink, wink) "erotic experiences" of her own.

Warm sensuous trade winds caress every move, azure blue waters entice and lubricate, the scent of tropical flowers intoxicate, and millions of crabs cover the beach.

A full Caribbean Moon dares you further, to experience full sensory overload, magical and erotic beyond belief.

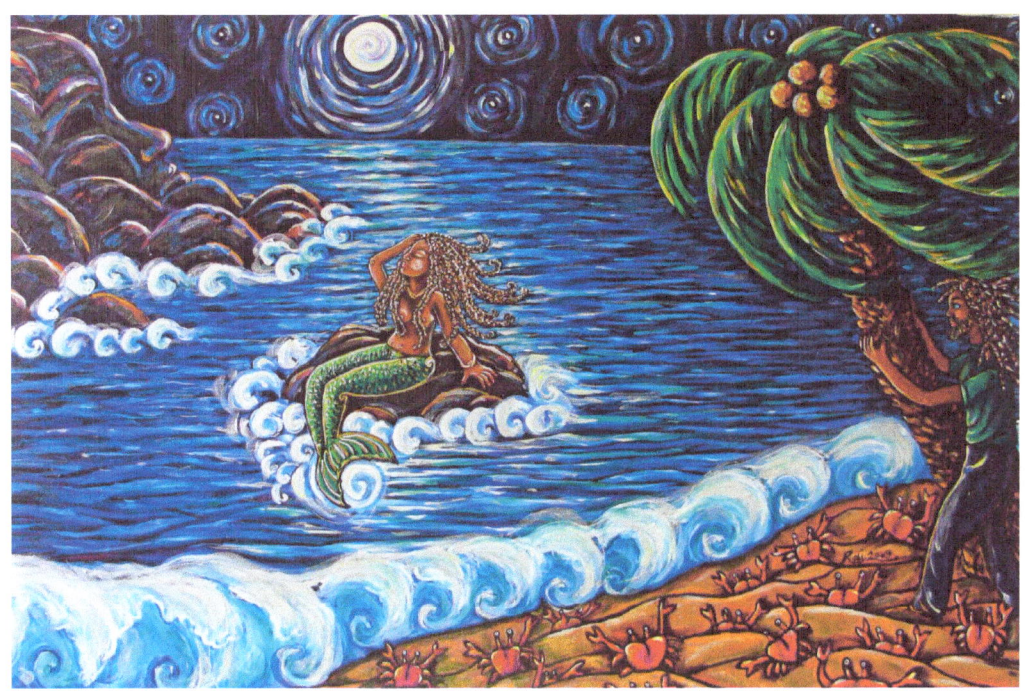

The Mermaid
Roxi Sim Hermsen
60"x39"
Acrylic on canvas

The magical Caribbean moonlight illuminates the sensuous mermaid;
he simply cannot believe his eyes...

Ryan Robson

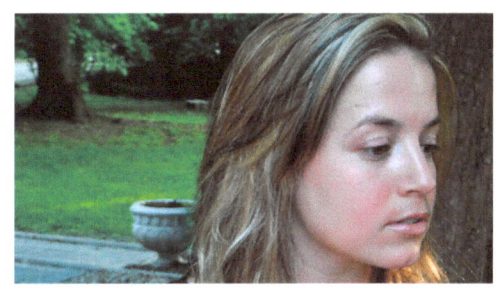

Sexual Digestion

I wipe my runny nose from my upper lip onto my hand while one thousand gorgeous faces stare back at me. My orifices leak as I question the representation of these women. If they are real than what am I? I, am bothered and quite bored of the constant comparison within the role dictated by my gender. Using bodily fluids as my palette I blend the subject with the ab-ject. To be vulnerable takes guys, thus I pull my guts out and play with them in front of you. I wipe nothing away leaving you with what you wish not to see. For my body and your body are non-stop sexual digestive machines, constantly pulling things in and pushing them out.

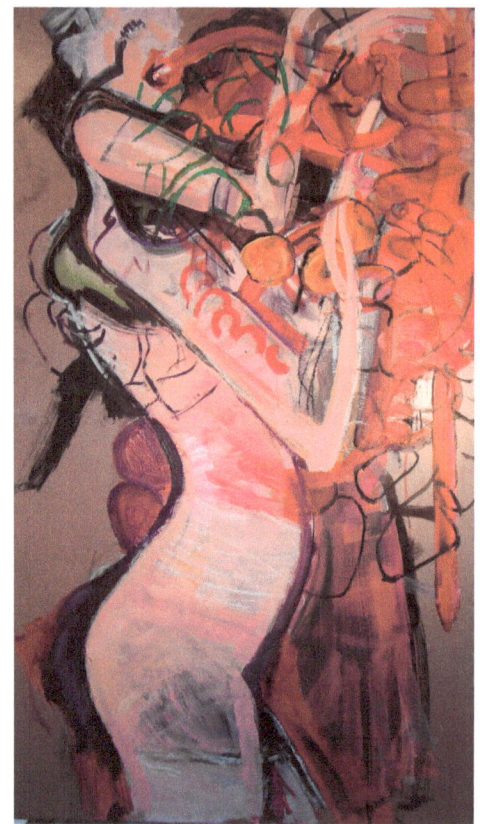

Inside Out Playground
Ryan Robson
34"x55"
Charcoal, acrylic, ink

Our body is the canvas and the fluids are the paint.

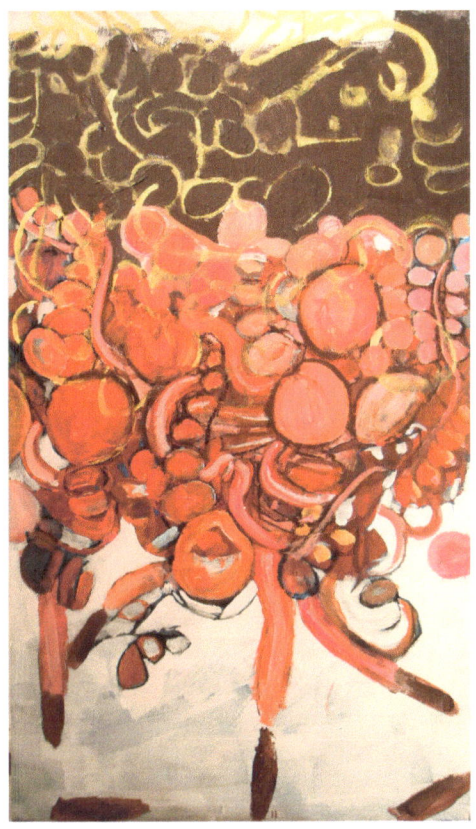

Digestive Pleasure
Ryan Robson
34"x55"
Charcoal, acrylic, ink

OOOO the pleasure of digestion, in and out, in and out, in and out.

Sandra Windsor

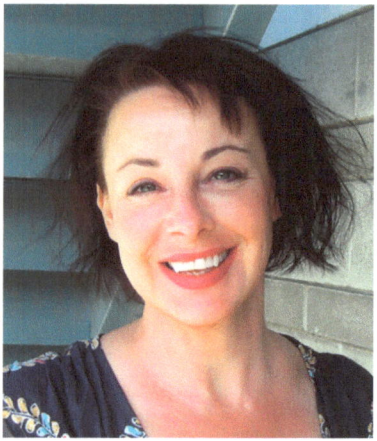

Sandra, or Sam if you like..... is a resident of Lake country .....at present. She grew up on the coast and has always had a passion for drawing, painting and dance. She is involved in flamenco dance and art modeling as well as creating paintings and drawings. Sandra comes from a family of painters and carvers. Her recent travels have taken her to Portugal and Spain... She enjoys the passion of the music, dance and the formal form of the art and architecture of these different countries. Twilight Solicitation's arrived from these experiences ....and she said..... " of course the primitive emotion of sensual passion"

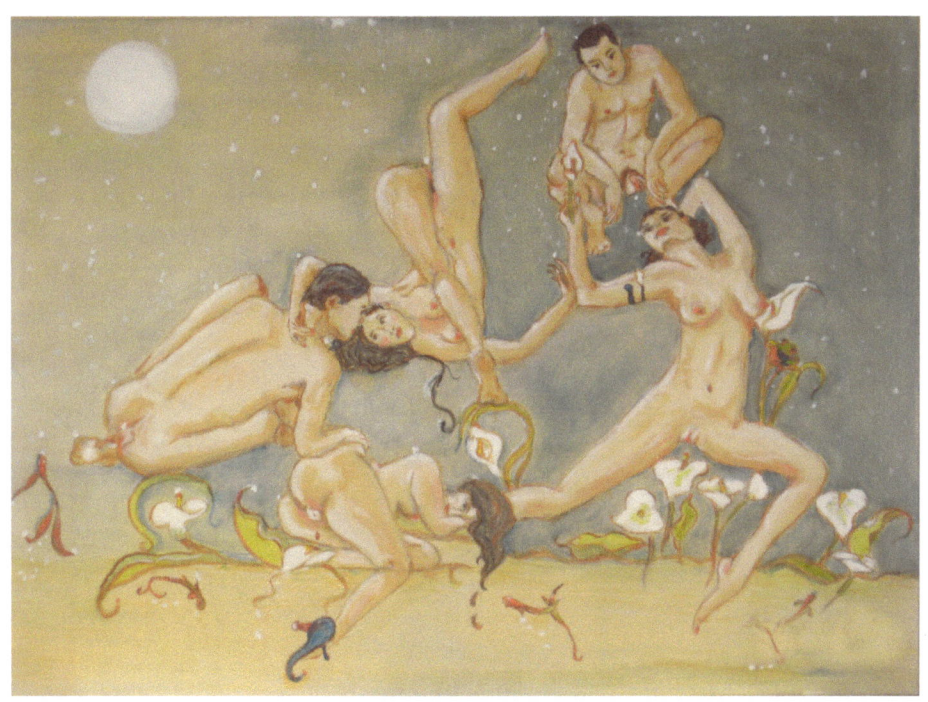

Twilight Solicitations
Sam Windsor
18"x24"
Acrylic on canvas

Twilight shelters knowing gazes.............
the longer you look the more you will see........... so linger and enjoy the fantasy.

Sea Dean

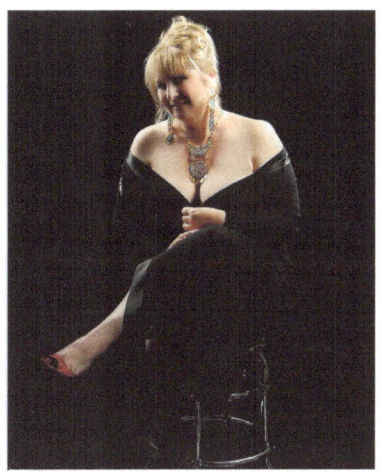

I was born and educated in England but I have called the Okanagan home for the last 35 years. Recently my life has radically changed after losing several people close to me and being seriously affected by the downturn in the economy. I like to think this has added depth to my work, but my irrepressible inner child will always shine through. I've worn many hats to pay bills but I've recently returned to creation and it is thoroughly cathartic. Out of darkness comes light.

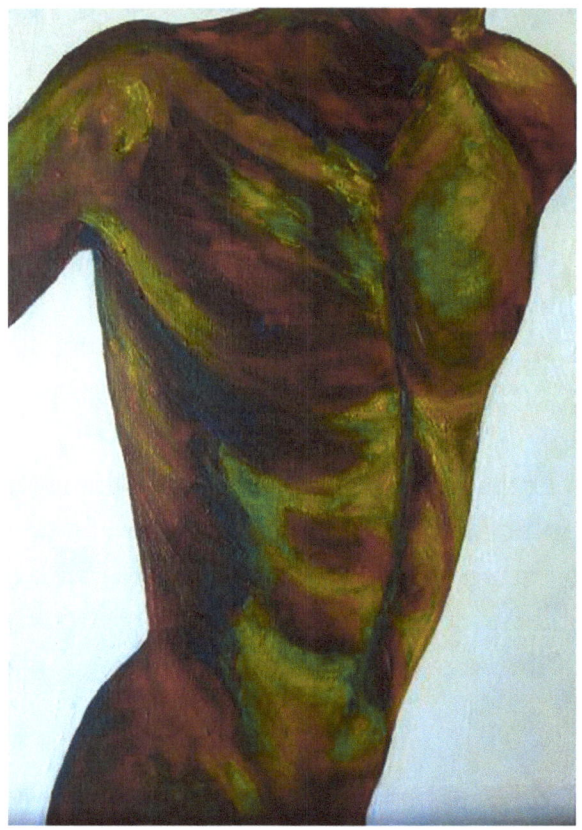

Chocolate
Sea Dean
10"x8"
Acrylic on Canvas Board

He is lithe and strong running free.
As he turns there is a moment of astonishment and excitement...

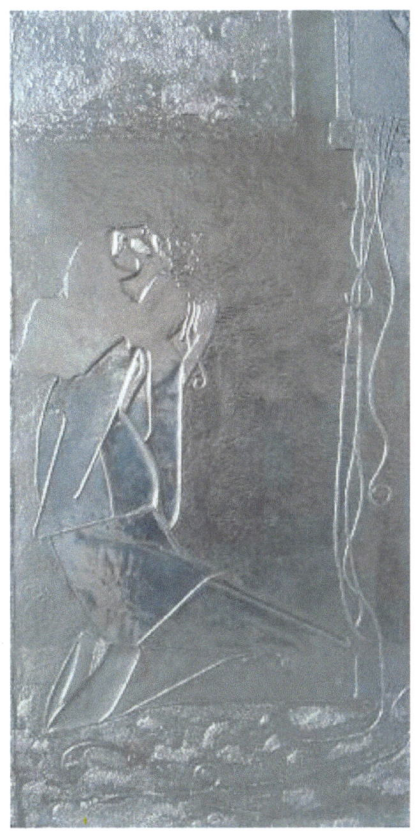

Japan
Sea Dean
23"x11"
Multi Media – Board, Resin, Foil

She sorrows for her passing love.
From darkness and despair comes light and life.
One small kindness will ignite her passion. Joy is only a heartbeat away.

Sharon Rose

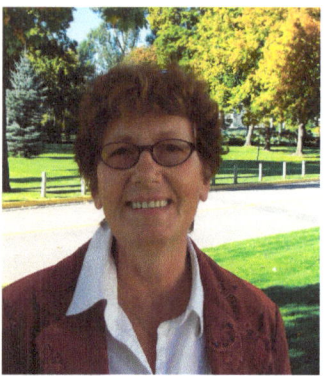

Sharon began working from life with the human form ten years ago and can now find no other subject that provides such challenge and excitement.

In her own words:

"Every changing thought is followed by a corresponding chemical change within the body and subtle changes in the body aura and physical appearance --- a never ending study --- Everything else, by comparison, becomes boring!"

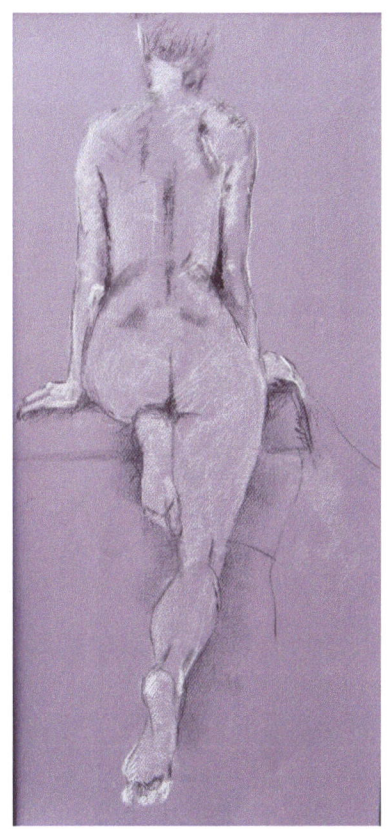

After
Sharon Rose
Vine Charcoal and conte

After
Moments of Splendor
Always to Remember
Moments of Regret
Trying to Forget
Moments of Flavor
Forever to Savor

Shirley Leswick

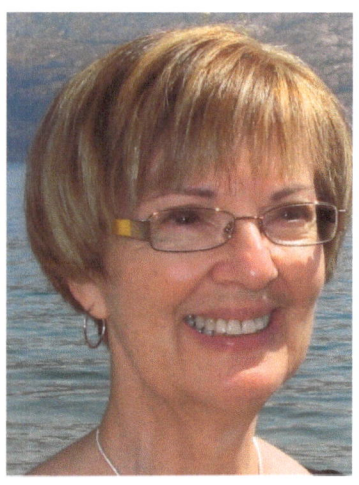

After retiring from her teaching career and moving with her husband to Kelowna, Shirley's interest in drawing and painting was rekindled. Over the past decade, her passion for art has grown as a result of her studies with several professional artists. She takes joy in creating both portraits and landscapes, and has received commissions from across North America. Shirley continues to be inspired by the beautiful surroundings here in the Okanagan, as well as by personal photos from her travels to the United States, Mexico, Asia, Europe, Australia and New Zealand. Although she works with graphite, watercolour and mixed media, her favourite medium remains pastel.

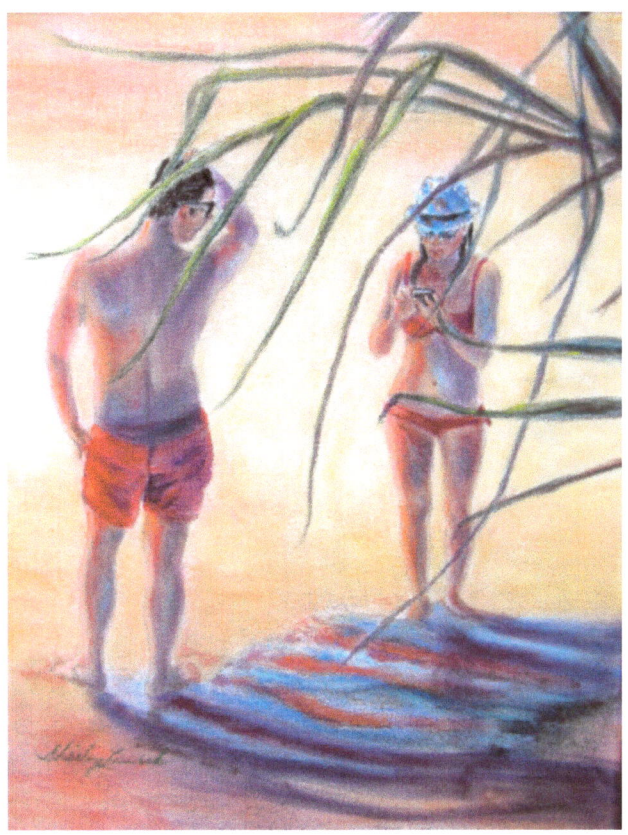

I'll be home late
Shirley Leswick
20"x16"
Pastel on canvas

As shadows lengthen and the temperature cools, heat rises within
him while he waits impatiently for her to finish her text....

Tina Aziz-Siddiqui

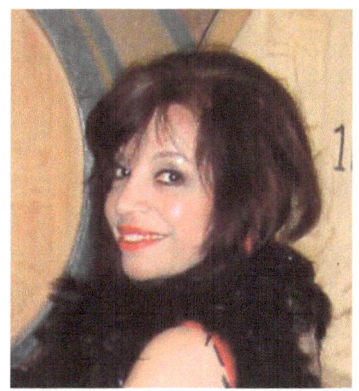

Multidimensional aspect of the human form continuously fascinates me hence my relentless quest to represent it in the various mediums I work in. Deconstruction of forms as I built up my collages is totally consuming as I work my way through composition, colour, form and light.

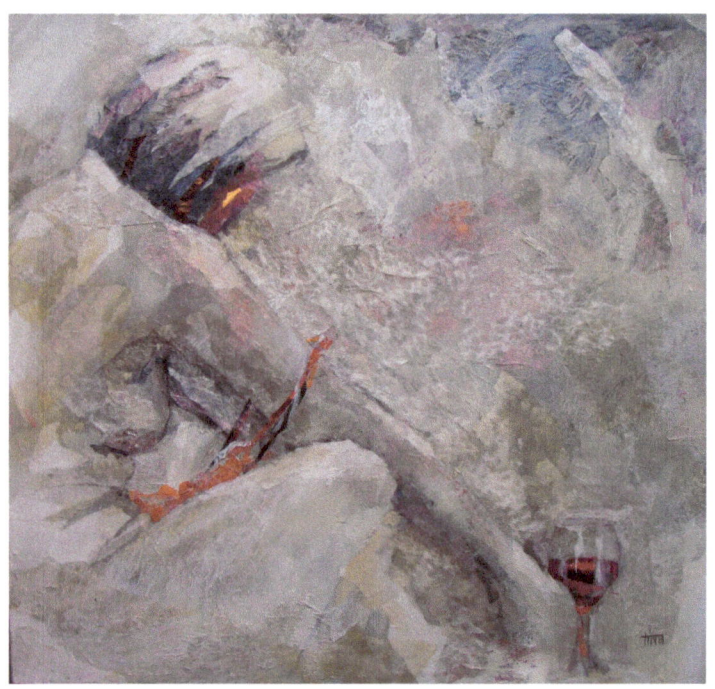

Surrender to the Night
Tina Aziz-Siddiqui
12"x12"
Collage on canvas

Every sip allures her deeper into the pleasure of the Night, she lets
her hair down ..... straps slips off her shoulders.......

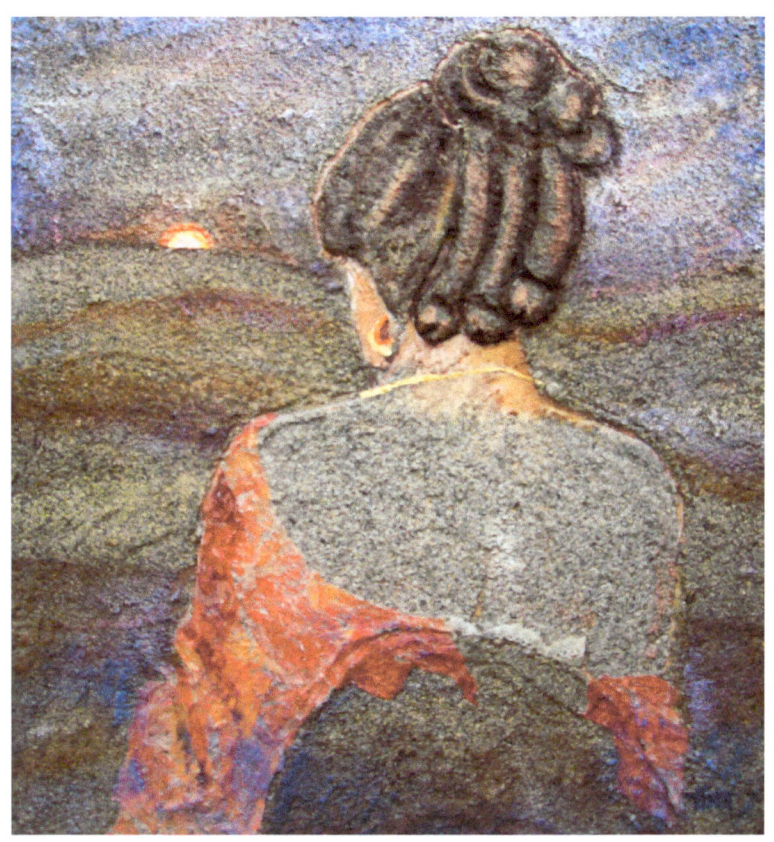

Demons in her head
Tina Aziz-Siddiqui
10"x8"
Mixed media on canvas

Her desert folks may accuse her of harbouring "demons" in her head
(genital shapes in her hair),yet she wonders
"When will the Viagra kick in?"

Trina Ganson

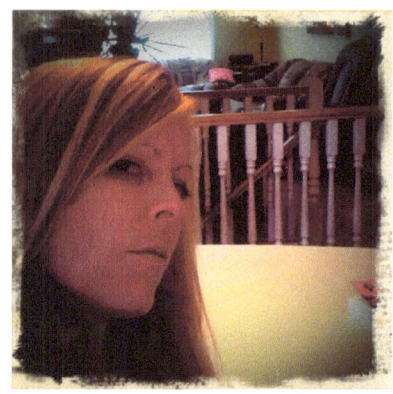

Trina Ganson is a printmaker and member of Studio 113. Trina received her Diploma in Fina Arts from the Okanagan University College in 2005. After a few years of focused art-making, Trina returned to the Okanagan to receive her BFA from the University of British Columbia Okanagan in 2008. Trina now teaches printmaking and continues the journey in her own work in the Rotary Centre for the Arts.

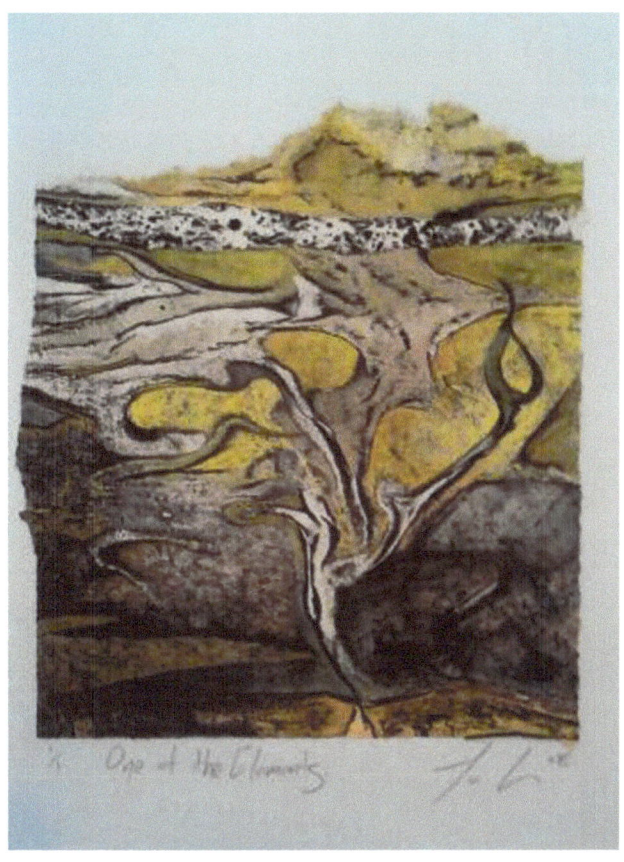

One of the Elements
Trina Ganson
10.5"x9.5"
Collograph with Drawing

I am mesmerized by the fabric of life, the fragility of its simplicity and its complexities. I am interested in how these elements are in the folds of this image, represented by a blending of shape, texture and colour that demands my attention and allows me to find new ways to respond with every glance.

So....

There you have it.

Another year for the Okanagan Erotic Show is complete.

I don't pretend to be a professional publisher or writer, but I do make a huge effort to acknowledge artists who participate in my shows. One way I do that is by the web site, another way is by the catalog. Catalogs give substantiation and solidity to an artist's work by saying it is important enough to be printed. I have the skills, and the knowledge, so why not... ?

All participating artists have the option and choice to be in the catalog, and they do not pay for inclusion. Being in this catalog is not a requirement for being in the show: there are three artists who were in the show, but who chose not to be in the catalog. There is even an artist who chose not to be on the web.
That is absolutely their right.

The Call for Artists will come out again in January 2012, with a deadline of May 31. I am quite thorough on the web site, and your answers are likely there. Please consider in sending in a submission, share the Call with your friends.

Maybe....

think about knocking our socks off.

See you next year.

Julia Trops

http://www.okanaganeroticartshow.com
http://www.facebook.com/EroticArtShow
http://www.exnihilovineyards.com
http://www.facebook.com/ExNihiloWine

www.ingramcontent.com/pod-product-compliance
Lightning Source LLC
Chambersburg PA
CBHW050716180526
45159CB00003B/1044